THE TURBULENT 60s

1966

**Other books in the
Turbulent 60s series:**

THE TURBULENT 60s

1966

Carol Carwile Head and Tom Head, *Book Editors*

Bruce Glassman, *Vice President*
Bonnie Szumski, *Publisher*
Scott Barbour, *Managing Editor*
David M. Haugen, *Series Editor*

**GREENHAVEN
PRESS**®

THOMSON
——✳——™
GALE

San Diego • Detroit • New York • San Francisco • Cleveland
New Haven, Conn. • Waterville, Maine • London • Munich

THOMSON
GALE

Dedication

For Cappy

LIBRARY OF CONGRESS CATALOGING-IN-PUBLICATION DATA

1966 / Carol Carwile Head, Tom Head, book editors.
   p. cm. — (The turbulent 60s)
Includes bibliographical references and index.
ISBN 0-7377-1836-6 (lib. bdg. : alk. paper) —
ISBN 0-7377-1837-4 (pbk. : alk. paper)
   1. United States—History—1961–1969—Sources. 2. A.D. nineteen sixty-six—Sources. I. Head, Carol Carwile. II. Head, Tom. III. Series.
E846.A183 2004
973.923—dc22
                                             2003056875

Printed in the United States of America

CONTENTS

T he 1960s were a period of immense change in America. What many view as the complacency of the 1950s gave way to increased radicalism in the 1960s. The newfound activism of America's youth turned an entire generation against the social conventions of their parents. The rebellious spirit that marked young adulthood was no longer a stigma of the outcast but rather a badge of honor among those who wanted to remake the world. And in the 1960s, there was much to rebel against in America. The nation's involvement in Vietnam was one of the catalysts that helped galvanize young people in the early 1960s. Another factor was the day-to-day Cold War paranoia that seemed to be the unwelcome legacy of the last generation. And for black Americans in particular, there was the inertia of the civil rights movement that, despite seminal victories in the 1950s, had not effectively countered the racism still plaguing the country. All of these concerns prompted the young to speak out, to decry the state of the nation that would be their inheritance.

The 1960s, then, may best be remembered for its spirit of confrontation. The student movement questioned American imperialism, militant civil rights activists confronted their elders over the slow progress of change, and the flower children faced the nation's capitalistic greed and conservative ethics and opted to create a counterculture. There was a sense of immediacy to all this activism, and people put their bodies on the line to bring about change. Although there were reactionaries and conservative holdouts, the general feeling was that a united spirit of resistance could stop the inevitability of history. People could shape their own destinies, and together they could make a better world. As sixties chronicler Todd Gitlin writes, "In the Sixties it seemed especially true that History with a capital H had come down to earth, either interfering with life or making it possible: and that within History, or threaded through it, people were living with a supercharged density: lives were bound up with one another, making claims on one another, drawing one another into the common project."

Perhaps not everyone experienced what Gitlin describes, but few would argue that the nation as a whole was left untouched by the radical notions of the times. The women's movement, the civil rights movement, and the antiwar movement left indelible marks. Even the hippie movement left behind a relaxed morality and a more ecological mindset. Popular culture, in turn, reflected these changes: Music became more diverse and experimental, movies adopted more adult themes, and fashion attempted to replicate the spirit of uninhibited youth. It seemed that every facet of American culture was affected by the pervasiveness of revolution in the 1960s, and despite the diversity of rebellions, there remained a sense that all were related to, as Gitlin puts it, "the common project."

Of course, this communal zeitgeist of the 1960s is best attributed to the decade in retrospect. The 1960s were not a singular phenomenon but a progress of individual days, of individual years. Greenhaven Press follows this rubric in The Turbulent Sixties series. Each volume of this series is devoted to the major events that define a specific year of the decade. The events are discussed in carefully chosen articles. Some of these articles are written by historians who have the benefit of hindsight, but most are contemporary accounts that reveal the complexity, confusion, excitement, and turbulence of the times. Each article is prefaced by an introduction that places the event in its historical context. Every anthology is also introduced by an essay that gives shape to the entire year. In addition, the volumes in the series contain time lines, each of which gives an at-a-glance structure to the major events of the topic year. A bibliography of helpful sources is also provided in each anthology to offer avenues for further study. With these tools, readers will better understand the developments in the political arena, the civil rights movement, the counterculture, and other facets of American society in each year. And by following the trends and events that define the individual years, readers will appreciate the revolutionary currents of this tumultuous decade—the turbulent sixties.

The Year of Escalation

During the year 1966, the United States faced increasing tension both at home and abroad. It was a year in which hundreds of thousands of young Americans were sent off to a war that was becoming more complex, more dangerous, and less popular. It was a year in which the civil rights movement, traditionally dominated by nonviolent leaders such as Martin Luther King Jr., became influenced by more militant ideals. It was a year in which women's liberation came of age, and feminists focused on gender discrimination in the workplace. Other events—such as the first large-scale successful protest on behalf of migrant farmworkers' rights and the first unmanned lunar landing—brought new controversies into the public consciousness. Although it could be said that the sixties as a whole made U.S. culture more complex and less innocent, many of the most important and divisive issues of that decade reached their boiling point in 1966.

The Vietnam War

As 1965 drew to a close, the conflict in Vietnam had begun to grow in size but retained significant public support. A poll taken in August showed that 61 percent of Americans supported the war and believed that victory was still a possibility. Ranks swelling with a new wave of draftees, the U.S. military had stationed about 184,000 soldiers in Vietnam as 1966 began.

Still, there were many who opposed the war. There seemed to be no clear objectives in Vietnam other than to stop the fall of South Vietnam. And not everyone was sure that the South Vietnamese government was a democracy worth saving. As U.S. casualty numbers gradually began to increase and troop commitment rose, President Lyndon Johnson and his military commanders found themselves waging a war that was becoming less and less popular. In his January 1966 State of the Union address, Johnson attempted to justify the continuing U.S. military intervention in Vietnam:

> And we will stay until aggression has stopped. We will stay because a just nation cannot leave to the cruelties of its enemies a people who have staked their lives and independence on America's solemn pledge. . . . We will stay because in Asia—and around the world—are countries whose independence rests, in large measure, on confidence in America's word and in America's protection. To yield to force in Vietnam would weaken that confidence, would undermine the independence of many lands, and would whet the appetite of aggression. We would have to fight in one land, and then we would have to fight in another— or abandon much of Asia to the domination of Communists.[1]

In February, Johnson met with South Vietnamese prime minister Nguyen Cao Ky and President Nguyen Van Thieu at the Honolulu Conference. In a joint declaration, Johnson's administration pledged to help the South Vietnamese government defeat the Vietcong guerrillas in South Vietnam and stop incursions from Communist North Vietnam. Johnson's administration supported this pledge by sending more troops; by the end of 1966, the number of U.S. soldiers in Vietnam had more than doubled from 184,000 to 389,000. To bolster the number of available troops, the Johnson administration tripled the number of draft calls from 10,000 to 30,000 per month, sparking widespread protests and resistance. Some draftees fled to Canada in an effort to escape the increasingly dangerous and unpopular war.

By October, the Johnson administration had become focused on ending the war by more realistic means. At the Manila Conference in the Philippines, Johnson met with representatives from Australia, New Zealand, the Philippines, South Korea, South Vietnam, and Thailand to draft a new strategy. Instead of banking on a purely military victory, as the Honolulu declaration had, the new Manila declaration listed a series of conditions that the North Vietnamese government could meet to end the war. In effect, Johnson was hoping that the north, fearful of a greater U.S. commitment, would sue for peace. Though North Vietnam showed willingness to negotiate, it was not awed by the American threat.

In the following month, the war became far less popular—public support dropped from 61 percent to 50 percent—and quick victory seemed an extremely unlikely prospect. U.S. military commanders became openly pessimistic about the chances of a conventional victory, but at the same time they felt compelled to increase the U.S. presence in hopes of avoiding defeat. During 1966, the Vietnam War had become a strategic nightmare—a war that leaders in the Johnson administration felt they could not win, lose, or quit.

The Rise of the Black Power Movement

As the United States faced increasing tension in Vietnam, new domestic controversies also began to take shape. On June 5, 1966, James Meredith—the first black student to attend the University of Mississippi ("Ole Miss")—began a solitary March Against Fear along 220 miles of roads and highway from Memphis, Tennessee, to Jackson, Mississippi, to encourage African Americans to vote. When he was shot and wounded en route by a white supremacist, the march was resumed by thousands led by Martin Luther King Jr. and a young activist named Stokely Carmichael. By the time the march reached Jackson on June 26, it had grown to thirty thousand strong.

After Carmichael arrived in Jackson, he delivered an angry speech to the assembled crowd. Carmichael was tired of the unavenged killings of blacks and the intolerably slow, white bureaucracy that kept promising civil rights in time. He called on African Americans to support each other and create political and economic "black power" in an effort to combat deep-seated institutional racism. In *Black Power*, which Carmichael cowrote later the same year with Lincoln University political science professor Charles V. Hamilton, the authors explained the term further:

> The concept of Black Power rests on a fundamental premise: *Before a group can enter the open society, it must first close ranks.* . . . Black people must lead and run their own organizations. Only black people can convey the revolutionary idea—and it is a revolutionary idea—that black people are able to do things themselves. Only they can help create in the community an aroused and continuing black consciousness that will provide the basis for political strength.[2]

Carmichael's concept of black power contrasted sharply with

the inclusive and conciliatory rhetoric of King and other civil rights activists of his time. Both the phrase and the idea of black power soon entered public consciousness and found favor with activists who had grown impatient with the inclusive but plodding civil rights movement.

One group that embraced similar ideas was the Black Panther Party for Self-Defense. Founded in October 1966 by activists Huey P. Newton and Bobby Seale, the organization encouraged its members to bear arms and forcibly protect African Americans from police abuse. Although the organization also sponsored a number of nonviolent initiatives, including school lunch programs and medical research, its confrontational tone and its exclusive focus on black membership alienated many mainstream civil rights activists.

The National Organization for Women

Also founded in October was the National Organization for Women (NOW), a civil rights group led by Betty Friedan, author of the best-selling and controversial *The Feminine Mystique* (1963). NOW would quickly become the most visible and credible women's rights organization of its time (and has remained so for several decades). In a speech Friedan gave to NOW in 1967, outlining its successes over the previous year, she argued that the organization had something unique to contribute to the national dialogue:

> Our first order of business was to make clear to Washington, to employers, to unions, and to the nation that someone *was* watching, someone *cared* about ending sex discrimination. . . . Unlike most women's organizations and official spokeswomen, we are not timid about taking our case to the nation through the mass media. For we know the importance of bringing the question of sex discrimination out from under the table, where it can be ignored or sniggered away, to confront the human rights consciousness and conscience of this country.[3]

One of the first causes NOW addressed was job discrimination. Under Title VII of the Civil Rights Act of 1964, employers and government agencies are prohibited from discriminating against employees or prospective employees on the basis of "race, color, religion, sex, or national origin." However, the U.S. Equal Employment Opportunity Commission (EEOC), the gov-

ernment agency responsible for enforcing Title VII, generally ignored sex discrimination complaints and permitted a number of
discriminatory policies. For example, newspapers sorted job listings by gender (under the categories of "Help Wanted—Male"
and "Help Wanted—Female"), airline companies fired flight attendants when they reached their thirties or got married, and
women serving in the armed forces were not granted full retire-
ment benefits.

NOW responded by staging well-publicized protests and,
when that failed, threatened to file a lawsuit against the U.S. government for refusing to enforce Title VII. In an effort to avoid a
high-profile lawsuit, the EEOC agreed to hearings with NOW
and began to enforce the sex discrimination clause. Newspapers
were required to integrate their job listings, and airline industry
standards discriminating against women were scrutinized. President Johnson would later sign executive orders granting full re-
tirement benefits to women serving in the military and banning
sex discrimination in government agencies and among government contractors.

Conflict and Resolution

The year 1966 was one of rising tensions and rising stakes, and
many of the most prominent events of the year were more oriented
toward the future than the present. The single event that dominated
the U.S. political climate was the Vietnam War, which transformed
in 1966 from a war perceived as practical and winnable to a
morass draining the country of resources and America's youth.

This increasing pressure was reflected even in happier events,
such as the founding of NOW and the success a migrant farmworkers' strike led by Cesar Chavez, because activists at the time
knew that these early successes represented only the first steps
in what would be a long and difficult struggle. As the sixties began to draw to a close, the tensions of 1966 would escalate even
further. The civil rights movement would become increasingly
polarized and antagonistic. The Vietnam War would become the
divisive issue that tore the nation apart. And the youth movement
that would turn 1967 into the Summer of Love would lose its in-
nocence in the Chicago riots of 1968. In 1966, however, the nation had yet to reach the breaking point.

Notes

1. Lyndon Johnson, State of the Union Address of President Johnson to the Congress, January 12, 1966.

2. Stokely Carmichael and Charles V. Hamilton, *Black Power: The Politics of Liberation in America.* New York: Random House, 1967, pp. 44–46.

3. Betty Friedan, *It Changed My Life: Writings on the Women's Movement.* New York: Random House, 1976, p. 98.

Cesar Chavez and the Delano Grape Strikes

By Cesar Chavez

Described as "one of the heroic figures of our time" by Senator Robert F. Kennedy, Presidential Medal of Freedom recipient Cesar Estrada Chavez was born March 31, 1927, on a small ranch near Yuma, Arizona. After his father lost the land as a result of an inability to pay taxes during the Great Depression, ten-year-old Cesar and his family became migrant farmworkers in various fields and vineyards throughout the Southwest.

As a Mexican American, Chavez faced racism as a child. He was aware of how poorly treated and underpaid his fellow migrants were. In 1945, he joined the U.S. Navy and served in the Western Pacific during the latter part of World War II. He had hoped to learn a skill in the navy, but racism dogged him even while serving his country. With few prospects after his discharge, Chavez returned to migrant labor.

In 1952, Chavez met an organizer for the Community Service Organization (CSO), a self-help group, and within several months became an organizer. By the late 1950s, he was the CSO national director. His dream, however, was to create a new organization to help farmworkers, because the CSO did not address that need. In 1962, he resigned his CSO position and moved with his wife and children to Delano, California, where he founded the National Farm Workers Association (NFWA). He and his wife once more worked in the fields as migrant workers, though Chavez also traveled to neighboring farm communities to organize farmworkers into the union. Chavez's hope was that, together, the migrant workers could fight for better living conditions and higher wages.

By September 1965, Chavez's group of migrant workers had changed its name to the United Farm Workers (UFW). The organization had grown to over twelve hundred member families and, in that year, organize with a group of migrant Filipino workers to strike against grape growers in California. In 1966, Chavez organized a march from Delano to Sacramento, California, the state capital, to bring government attention to *la causa*—the cause. Before the march, Chavez issued the "Sacramento March Letters" so that workers and the general public would know the reason for the protest. During the march, another tract called "The Plan of Delano" was read and distributed in English and Spanish at every evening gathering as well as at many other gatherings throughout the pilgrimage. Both of these documents are reprinted below.

The "grape strike" lasted until 1970, when the most powerful produce growers in the United States agreed to the union's demands. It was the first of many UFW events that improved working conditions for farmworkers throughout the United States. Like Mohandas Gandhi and Martin Luther King Jr., Chavez was committed to the philosophy of nonviolent resistance. He was jailed several times, and even from behind bars he led *la causa* with inspirational words and debilitating hunger strikes.

Cesar Chavez died in 1993 while serving as president of the United Farm Workers of America, the first successful national farmworkers' union in U.S. history.

Sacramento March Letter, March 1966

In the "March from Delano to Sacramento" there is a meeting of cultures and traditions; the centuries-old religious tradition of Spanish culture conjoins with the very contemporary cultural syndromes of "demonstration" springing from the spontaneity of the poor, the downtrodden, the rejected, the discriminated-against baring visibly their need and demand for equality and freedom.

In every religious orientated culture "the pilgrimage" has had a place, a trip made with sacrifice and hardship as an expression of penance and of commitment—and often involving a petition to the patron of the pilgrimage for some sincerely sought benefit of body or soul. Pilgrimage has not passed from Mexican culture. Daily at any of the major shrines of the country, and in particular at the Basilica of the Lady of Guadalupe there arrive pilgrims from all points—some of whom may have long since walked-out the pieces of rubber tire that once served them as soles, and many of whom will walk on their knees the last mile or so of the pilgrimage. Many of the "pilgrims" of Delano will have walked such pilgrimages themselves in their lives—perhaps as very small children even; and cling to the memory of the day-long marches, the camps at night, streams forded, hills climbed, the sacral aura of the sanctuary and the "fiesta" that followed.

But throughout the Spanish speaking world there is another tradition that touches the present march, that of the Lenten penitential processions, where the penitentes would march through the streets, often in sack cloth and ashes, some even carrying crosses as a sign of penance for their sins, and as a plea for the mercy of God. The penitential procession is also in the blood of the Mexican American, and the Delano march will therefore be one of penance—public penance for the sins of the strikers, their own personal sins as well as their yielding perhaps to feelings of hatred and revenge in the strike itself. They hope by the march to set themselves at peace with the Lord, so that the justice of their cause will be purified of all lesser motivation.

These two great traditions of a great people meet in the Mexican American with the belief that Delano is his "cause," his great demand for justice, freedom, and respect from a predominantly foreign cultural community in a land where he was first. The revolutions of Mexico were primarily uprisings of the poor, fighting for bread and for dignity. The Mexican American is also a child of the revolution.

Pilgrimage, penance and revolution. The pilgrimage from Delano to Sacramento has strong religio-cultural overtones. But it is also the pilgrimage of a cultural minority who have suffered from a hostile environment, and a minority who means business.

The Plan of Delano

PLAN for the liberation of the Farm Workers associated with the Delano Grape Strike in the State of California, seeking social justice in farm labor with those reforms that they believe necessary for their well-being as workers in these United States.

We the undersigned, gathered in Pilgrimage to the capital of the State in Sacramento in penance for all the failings of Farm Workers, as free and sovereign men, do solemnly declare before the civilized world which judges our actions, and before the nation to which we belong, the propositions we have formulated to end the injustice that oppresses us.

We are conscious of the historical significance of our Pilgrimage. It is clearly evident that our path travels through a valley well known to all Mexican farm workers. We know all of these towns of Delano, Madera, Fresno, Modesto, Stockton and Sacramento, because along this very same road, in this very same valley, the Mexican race has sacrificed itself for the last hundred years. Our sweat and our blood have fallen on this land to make other men rich. This Pilgrimage is a witness to the suffering we have seen for generations.

The Penance we accept symbolizes the suffering we shall have in order to bring justice to these same towns, to this same valley. The Pilgrimage we make symbolizes the long historical road we have traveled in this valley alone, and the long road we have yet to travel, with much penance, in order to bring about the Revolution we need, and for which we present the propositions in the following PLAN:

1. This is the beginning of a social movement in fact and not in pronouncements. We seek our basic, God-given rights as human beings. Because we have suffered—and are not afraid to suffer—in order to survive. We are ready to give up everything, even our lives in our fight for social justice. We shall do it without violence because that is our destiny. To the ranchers, and to all those who oppose us, we say, in the words of Benito Juarez, "EL RESPETO AL DERECHO AJENO ES LA PAZ" ["respect of other people's rights is peace"].

2. We seek the support of all political groups and protection of the government, which is also our government, in our struggle. For too many years we have been treated like the lowest of the low. Our wages and working conditions have been determined from above, because irresponsible legislators who could have helped us, have supported the ranchers' argument that the plight of the Farm Worker was a "special case." They saw the obvious effects of an unjust system, starvation wages, contractors,

day hauls, forced migration, sickness, illiteracy, camps and sub-human living conditions, and acted is if they were irremediable causes. The farm worker has been abandoned to his own fate—without representation, without power—subject to mercy and caprice of the rancher. We are tired of words, of betrayals, of indifference. To the politicians we say that the years are gone when the farm worker said nothing and did nothing to help himself. From this movement shall spring leaders who shall understand us, lead us, be faithful to us, and we shall elect them to represent us. WE SHALL BE HEARD.

3. We seek, and have, the support of the Church in what we do. At the head of the Pilgrimage we carry LA VIRGEN DE LA GUADALUPE (the Virgin of Guadalupe) because she is ours, all ours, Patroness of the Mexican people. We also carry the Sacred Cross and the Star of David because we are not sectarians, and because we ask the help and prayers of all religions. All men are brothers—sons of the same God; that is why we say to all men of good will, in the words of Pope Leo XIII, "Everyone's first duty is to protect the workers from the greed of speculators who use human beings as instruments to provide themselves with money. It is neither just nor human to oppress men with excessive work to the point where their minds become enfeebled and their bodies worn out." GOD SHALL NOT ABANDON US.

4. We are suffering. We have suffered, and we are not afraid to suffer in order to win our cause. We have suffered unnumbered ills and crimes in the name of the law of the land. Our men, women, and children have suffered not only the basic brutality of stoop labor, and the most obvious injustices of the system; they have also suffered the desperation of knowing that that system caters to the greed of callous men and not to our needs. Now we will suffer for the purpose of ending the poverty, the misery, and the injustice, with the hope that our children will not be exploited as we have been. They have imposed hungers on us, and now we hunger for justice. We draw our strength from the very despair in which we have been forced to live. WE SHALL ENDURE.

5. We shall unite. We have learned the meaning of UNITY. We know why these United States are just that—united. The strength of the poor is also in union. We know that the poverty of the Mexican or Filipino worker in California is the same as that of all farm workers across the country, the Negroes and poor whites, the Puerto Ricans, Japanese, and Arabians; in short, all of the

races that comprise the oppressed minorities of the United States. The majority of the people on our Pilgrimage are of Mexican descent, but the triumph of our race depends on a national association of all farm workers. The ranchers want to keep us divided in order to keep us weak. Many of us have signed individual "work contracts" with the ranchers or contractors, contracts in which they had all the power. These contracts were farces, one more cynical joke at our impotence. That is why we must get together and bargain collectively. We must use the only strength that we have, the force of our numbers. The ranchers are few; we are many. UNITED WE SHALL STAND.

6. We will strike. We shall pursue the REVOLUTION we have proposed. We are sons of the Mexican Revolution, a revolution of the poor seeking bread and justice. Our revolution will not be armed, but we want the existing social order to dissolve; we want a new social order. We are poor, we are humble, and our only choice is to strike in those ranches where we are not treated with the respect we deserve as working men, where our rights as free and sovereign men are not recognized. We do not want the paternalism of the rancher, we do not want the contractor; we do not want charity at the price of our dignity. We want to be equal with all the working men in the nation; we want a just wage, better working conditions, a decent future for our children. To those who oppose us, be they ranchers, police, politicians, or speculators, we say that we are going to continue fighting until we die, or we win. WE SHALL OVERCOME.

Across the San Joaquin Valley, across California, across the entire Southwest of the United States, wherever there are Mexican people, wherever there are farm workers, our movement is spreading like flames across a dry plain. Our PILGRIMAGE is the MATCH that will light our cause for all farm workers to see what is happening here, so that they may do as we have done. The time has come for the liberation of the poor farm workers.

History is on our side.

MAY THE STRIKE GO ON! VIVA LA CAUSA [long live the cause]!

Amateur Computer Society Founded

By Stephen B. Gray

"If you could find a specific date for the birth of personal computing," wrote computer engineer and technical author Sol Libes in a 1978 article, "it would be May 5, 1966. For it was on that date that Stephen B. Gray founded the Amateur Computer Society and began publishing a quarterly called the *ACS Newsletter.*" Although Gray disagrees with this assessment, it would be fair to say that the ACS was at least the birth of the personal computing *movement.* In 1966, it was virtually impossible for one person to buy a ready-made computer. Anyone interested in building one had to rely on schematics printed in textbooks, building their own circuit boards from scratch at great effort and with very little support. This changed with the ACS, which for nine years provided a support network for amateur computer builders and made it possible for interested laypersons to build the same sorts of computers that professional engineers had been building.

In 1975, electronics manufacturers began selling computer "kits," which meant that amateur computer enthusiasts no longer had to build their own circuit boards. Having served its purpose, the Amateur Computer Society dissolved soon thereafter. Gray went on to have a highly successful career as a technical author, writing sixteen books on a wide range of computer-related topics. For its part, the Amateur Computer Society was the model for computer users' groups to come, and its newsletter is now housed by the Smithsonian Institution as a historical artifact from the earliest days of personal computing.

Stephen B. Gray, "The Early Days of Personal Computers," *Creative Computing*, November 1984. Copyright © 1984 by Ziff-Davis Publishing Company. Reproduced by permission.

In this 1984 article, Stephen B. Gray reflects on his experiences as founder of the ACS.

Twenty years ago, while I was the computers editor on *Electronics* magazine at McGraw-Hill, I realized there was much I could learn from building a computer. It didn't take long to find out how difficult it was just to get started. There were no kits, no "cookbooks." Computer textbooks usually contained partial schematics, but none told how to connect the various sections.

After several years of trying to build a digital computer in my spare time, I began to realize how difficult it must be for other hobbyists. So, to solicit information to help me build a machine and to share what little information I had been able to learn on my own, I sent a letter to seven electronics and computer trade magazines and three hobby publications on May 5, 1966:

> This is an invitation to those readers who are building their own computers to join the Amateur Computer Society, a nonprofit group open to anyone interested in building and operating a digital computer that will at least perform automatic multiplication and division, or is of a comparable complexity.
>
> The society publishes a bimonthly newsletter containing problems and answers, information about where to get parts and schematics and cheap ICs [integrated circuits], and articles on subjects such as Teletype equipment and checking out magnetic cores.
>
> Will interested readers please write to me, giving details on their proposed or in-the-works computers, such as word length, number of instructions, sources of parts and schematics, clever solutions to previous problems, etc.?

Response to the Letter

Five of the magazines printed some or all of the letter, and responses began to arrive. The original idea of the Amateur Computer Society, or ACS, was a membership organization with chapters and a newsletter or two. But the people who wrote in were so widely scattered that local chapters never got beyond the idea stage.

Initially, more than 160 men (but not one woman) wrote from

five countries and 27 states, and 110 eventually became early "members" of the ACS, although the most they got was the newsletter—$3 for the 11 issues in the first volume, from August 1966 to December 1968; $3 for the 12 issues of Volume II, from April 1969 to March 1972; and $5 for the 15 issues of Volume III, from June 1972 to June 1976. Only two issues of Volume IV were published: August and December 1976; the ACS Newsletter was then discontinued, with these words:

> Times have changed, and now that kits are so prevalent, there are other publications that serve the readers' purpose better than the *ACS Newsletter.* Also, the *ACS Newsletter* always depended heavily upon reader input, and this input has dwindled. . . . Thank you for your support over the last 10-½ years. It was fun while it lasted.

ACS membership never totalled more than a few hundred. Nor did I try actively to increase the number, because of the work involved in producing even a few hundred copies of each issue in my spare time. I was doing all the work, including typing, collating, folding, stuffing, and stamping. Had there been enough potential advertisers, the newsletter might have been turned into a magazine, but up until 1974 (and even later) there weren't enough to permit starting up a magazine devoted to computer-building.

Each of the first half dozen issues of the *ACS Newsletter* was devoted mostly to an individual topic such as sources of schematics, input/output, (mainly Teletype [TTY, a form of keyboard input/output]), logic circuits, memory, designing a computer kit for the ACS, mounting and interconnections, reference sources (where to find articles and books about computers), etc.

Responses from prospective members ranged all the way from "I've been thinking about building a computer for some time" (two dozen of these) through "I have the shift registers completed" (a dozen of these) to "I've build a computer and am now programming it" (two of these).

Building a Computer in 1966

Back in the mid-sixties, to build a simple computer accumulator, which could do no more than add successive inputs, using toggle switches for input and lamps for output, cost several dollars per bit. To build an extremely simple "computer" with four-bit words and without memory, and which divided the easy way (by repeated subtraction without shifting), could cost two or three hundred dollars.

Used vacuum tube computers were occasionally available, but such machines brought with them problems of size, power requirements, air-conditioning, and tube replacement costs.

Used transistor computers were seldom available at a price a hobbyist could afford; a Recomp III, even at five percent of its original cost, was still $4750. The cheapest third generation computer was still expensive; a PDP-8/E, made by Digital Equipment Corp., cost $5000 without a Teletype.

Building one's own computer was such a complicated undertaking that very few were ever completed, and nearly all of those were built by electronics engineers working in the data processing industry.

The main problem in building a computer was (and still is) the many technologies involved. Computer companies had specialists in logic, input/output, core memory, mass memory, peripherals, and other areas. To build one's own computer required learning a great deal about each one.

If the computer hobbyist was an electronics engineer working for a computer manufacturer, he could drop in on a friend down the hall or in the next building and ask what kind of drivers might be needed for a core memory with such-and-such specs. Most hobbyists had no such resources.

In addition to having to learn a great deal about computer electronics, the hobbyist also had to get into mechanical areas such as packaging, back-plane wiring, metal working, plastics, and many others. . . .

The Average ACS Computer

In the seventh issue of the *ACS Newsletter*, dated November 1967, a survey form was included asking for details of each member's computer, whether in the works or only in the planning stages. The next newsletter gave the survey results.

Most of those who returned the survey form planned on using core memory, the hardest part of the computer to get working; most wanted 4K [four thousand] or 8K words, but few got core up and running.

Teletype was the most common input/output device. Some members also used paper tape, Nixie readout tubes, magnetic tape, and electromechanical typewriters.

Clock speeds of the amateur computers averaged 0.5 MHz.

Generally speaking, beginning amateurs hoped to use a large number of instructions, between 50 and 100. Those who had gotten fairly well into the construction used no more than 11 to 34.

The average length of data words and instruction words was 12 bits for each. The speed required for addition ranged from eight microseconds down to ten milliseconds.

The number of registers ranged from two to 11, with three the most popular. One member projected two registers for memory, two for data, one for operation code, and five for address.

As to "cost so far," the range was from zero to $1500, with an average (among those reporting a cost) of $650. For "estimated cost when complete," the range was from $300 to "over $10,000," with an average of $2100. . . .

Many non-engineer ACS members, unable to design their own computers, tried copying existing designs. Several patterned their instruction set after that of the IBM 1401 or IBM 1620 computer. One Long Island member had software similar to that of the 1620 and hoped that his "IBM 1620 Model III" would be about 25 percent faster than IBM's 1620 Mod II, and would have all of its 60-plus instructions.

Most members who borrowed an instruction set already in use were copying that of the PDP-8 family, manufactured by Digital Equipment Corp. By that time, DEC had sold more than 10,000 of the PDP-8, which was attractive because of its comparatively low price, variety of programs available, and a simple yet powerful set of instructions.

Only two of those surveyed reported being anywhere near completion of their computers.

Jim Sutherland, an engineer with Westinghouse in Pittsburgh, noted that his Echo IV took a year to build and would need ten years to program. Echo IV was seven feet long, one and a half feet deep, and six feet high. The central processor was complete but, as with all amateur computers, the input/output system was still growing. . . .

The *ACS Newsletter*

The first volume of the *ACS Newsletter* (1966–68) provided information about computer trainers, Teletype equipment, circuit boards, ICs, kits, and details of computers built by members. The second volume (1969–72) included information about Nixie read-out tubes, core memory, buying reject ICs, memory drums, and the MITS desk calculator kit. It also described the first commercial computer kit, the National Radio Institute NRI 832 (1971). . . .

Volume III (1972–76) looked into Don Tarbell's computer (which multiplied a 140-digit number by itself in 40 seconds), Intel's 4004, and 8008 chips, the Scelbi-8H kit, Radio-Electronics Mark-8 kit, Hal Chamberlain's HAL-4096 computer, and several of the early commercial kits and boards. Only two issues were published of Volume IV in 1976; these dealt exclusively with commercial kits and peripherals as well as several products shown at the first personal computing show in Atlantic City.

A Flattering Accolade

An article by Sol Libes on "The First Ten Years of Amateur Computing" (*Byte*, July 1978, pp. 64–71) was taken largely from items in the *ACS Newsletter.* Written "to set the record straight," because many people thought personal computing "started only two or three years ago, with the introduction of the Altair 8800 by MITS," it continued:

> If one could find a specific date for the birth of personal computing, it would be May 5, 1966. For it was on that date that Stephen B. Gray founded the Amateur Computer Society and began publishing a quarterly called the *ACS Newsletter.*

Very flattering, but not true; it was like saying Henry Ford was the father of the automobile. If anything, the *ACS Newsletter* was the first publication in the world about personal computers. Apparently it is also the only detailed source about the early days; the Smithsonian Institution has asked for a set of the newsletters.

Surveyor 1 Lands on the Moon

By Homer E. Newell

By the time the sixties began, international politics was dominated by a Cold War between the two most powerful nations on Earth: the United States, committed to capitalism and democracy, and the Union of Soviet Socialist Republics (USSR), committed to the socialist ideal. This Cold War was, in many ways, a battle over the hearts and minds of the world. The U.S.-Soviet "space race" pitted the two nations against each other in a rivalry to become the first nation to master the domain of space. By 1966, the USSR was clearly winning this rivalry. Not only had the USSR been the first to launch a man-made satellite—*Sputnik*, in 1957—but also became the first to launch a human being into space when Yuri Gagarin's *Vostok I* orbited Earth in April 1961. The United States was, it seemed, the less technologically advanced nation; it had lost a great deal of international prestige and began to look to many like a weaker nation than the USSR.

One month after Gagarin's voyage, U.S. president John F. Kennedy committed the U.S. budget to defeating the Soviets in the space race in the most decisive way possible. "I believe," announced Kennedy, "that this nation should commit itself to achieving the goal, before this decade is out, of landing a man on the Moon and returning him safely to the Earth." The rate of progress was phenomenal; between 1961 and 1966, the United States launched eighteen manned flights into space as part of its Mercury and Gemini programs in an effort to test and perfect spacecraft equipment, all while launching unmanned spacecraft to ob-

Homer E. Newell, "Surveyor: Candid Camera on the Moon," *National Geographic Magazine*, October 1966. Copyright © 1966 by National Geographic Society. Reproduced by permission.

tain detailed photographs of the Moon. Actually *landing* on the Moon, however, was another prospect entirely.

On February 3, 1966, the Soviet *Luna IX* became the first spacecraft to land safely on the lunar surface in preparation for a manned lunar mission. On June 2, the American *Surveyor 1* became the second. Over the next two weeks, *Surveyor 1* broadcast over eleven thousand high-resolution photographs of the Moon's surface to Earth, where they were studied with an eye toward safely landing a manned spacecraft later. Six more Surveyor spacecraft were launched over the next eighteen months as a predecessor to the Apollo program, which landed a man safely on the Moon in July 1969, outrunning the USSR and redeeming America's reputation in the Cold War.

In this 1966 *National Geographic* article, NASA administrator Homer E. Newell describes the first Surveyor mission.

T oday, on a gray and desolate plain of the moon's Ocean of Storms, Surveyor I stands lifeless, a solitary artifact of men who live on another body of the solar system, 240,000 miles away.

Surveyor proved its ability to survive the furnace heat of the lunar noon, then go through the deep freeze of the 14-day-long lunar night at temperatures nearly 500 degrees colder, and still operate.

But now its batteries are dead; its antennas are useless; its solar panel and cyclopean camera eye stare blindly.

Surveyor I is silent, but in its brief life its performance far surpassed our hopes. By television it sent us more than 11,000 splendid pictures from the moon, including the first color photographs. It gave us a remarkably clear and intimate view of the lunar face, so close that we can measure and count particles only a fiftieth of an inch across. It even provided us with a glimpse beneath the moon's surface.

For the first time, because of Surveyor, Project Apollo officials feel real assurance that an astronaut can safely set foot on the moon, that the moon's surface will support him, and that he will not be swallowed up in a thick sea of dust.

Further, Surveyor added substantially to our meager knowledge of earth's natural satellite—information that we will be analyzing and digesting for months to come.

Even more, as Robert Parks, Surveyor Project Manager at the Jet Propulsion Laboratory in Pasadena, California, has pointed out, "The spacecraft gave us an engineering miracle. Its flight and landing worked exactly as expected. On its journey and on the moon, it answered almost flawlessly more than 100,000 radio commands sent principally through our huge antenna at Goldstone, in California's Mojave Desert."

We also used similar antennas near Johannesburg, South Africa, and at Tidbinbilla, near Canberra, Australia.

Surveyor Aim Only Nine Miles Off

Consider, for example, Surveyor I's accuracy. It was launched May 30, 1966, from a point on earth rotating at about 870 miles an hour, at a target moving some 2,300 miles an hour. Sixty-three hours and 36 minutes later, after traveling almost a quarter of a million miles, and with only one minor correction during its flight, it landed within nine miles of its target on the west side of the moon, close to the lunar equator.

Stephen E. Dwornik, Program Scientist for Surveyor, esti-

President John F. Kennedy addresses Congress on May 25, 1961, stating his commitment to landing a man on the moon and returning him safely to Earth.

mates that an expert rifleman firing at a fast-moving bull's-eye 250 yards away would have to hit within the thickness of this magazine to do as well.

Once in the vicinity of the moon, Surveyor's ultrasensitive radar began feeding to its self-contained computer information about its velocity and altitude. The main retrorocket, triggered by the altitude-marking radar, slowed the spacecraft's hurtling descent from 5,800 miles an hour to 290 miles an hour in 40 seconds. Then, small vernier rocket engines almost stopped it a few feet above the surface. Like some giant insect with its spindly legs spread wide, Surveyor fell the last 13 feet with half the speed of a parachute jumper—approximately 10 feet a second.

The three-legged robot, weighing about 600 pounds on earth but only about 100 in the moon's lower gravity, bounced slightly, oscillated briefly as its shock absorbers settled, and came to rest undamaged. Its footpads, 12-inch-diameter disks of crushable aluminum honeycomb, dug about an inch into the lunar surface.

At impact, the tubular aluminum legs pivoted to absorb shock, and crushable pads under the "knees" of the legs sank momentarily into the surface. . . .

What Surveyor saw after it landed was, of course, not totally new. Three Ranger spacecraft had sent back pictures just before crashing into the moon's face. Russia's Luna 9 landed on the moon last February and took a handful of close-up photographs.

But Surveyor saw with a sharper and clearer eye. And, for the first time, it saw in color. Three separate photographs, taken with orange, green, and blue filters, combined to produce a fairly accurate color representation. As scientists expected, that color seems to be nothing but gray—a plain, neutral gray.

Surveyor had but a single eye, its TV camera. Instead of turning this eye about, it gazed upward at a motor-driven mirror that, on radio command from earth, searched the ground below or scanned the horizon in almost a full circle.

The camera saw approximately as far as a man's eye would see, since the mirror was about 5½ feet above the surface. The horizon, because of the small diameter and sharp curvature of the moon, lay only about a mile away. On earth the horizon would have been roughly four miles distant.

And what did Surveyor see in the Ocean of Storms? It found itself in a shallow crater some 60 miles across. It had landed on a dark, level, relatively smooth spot. Low-lying hills and mountains of the crater's rim, at least 10 miles distant, poked their crests above the horizon.

Surveyor Settles an Old Controversy

In every direction stretched an eerie wasteland, scarred with smaller craters from an inch to several hundred feet across and littered with debris. Coarse blocks of rock as wide as three feet and countless smaller fragments lay strewn upon the crater lips and the surrounding areas.

The blocks and fragments represent debris ejected by the constant barrage of meteorites cratering the moon's surface, or rubble thrown out of secondary craters created by the impact of the original flying debris.

If all goes well, Surveyor I will have been followed by Surveyor II, next in a series of 10 planned missions. These will examine potential Apollo landing sites and survey other areas.

Lunar Orbiter I also may have flown, whirling round the moon to obtain photographs at altitudes as low as 30 miles and transmit back to earth pictures of potential Apollo and Surveyor landing zones. But so well did our first lunar soft-lander work that many scientists doubt that its successors will radically change our impression of the surface of the moon's vast "ocean" plains.

Before Surveyor I's voyage, scientists had engaged in intense speculation and prolonged controversy over the nature of the moon's face. Some argued firmly that the moon was covered with a deep blanket of soft dust. Others maintained just as vigorously that the surface was hard rock. Still others suggested spongy rock, or perhaps a thin covering of dust over rock.

Ranger's pictures did little to settle this controversy, for they were unable to resolve surface details smaller than 18 inches. A good many scientists tended to see in them what they hoped to see.

Surveyor changed all this. Now we know that, at least in one place in the Ocean of Storms, little if any loose dust threatens the Apollo astronauts. At the same time, the moon's surface seems not to consist of hard rock. Instead, scientists who study the Surveyor pictures find a layer of material that looks and behaves much like earthly soil. Judging by the shapes of small craters and the materials thrown up on their rims, we believe this layer may be as much as three feet thick. We think that essentially this same kind of material exists over a very large part of the moon's face, harrowed and worked and broken down by the incessant rain of meteorites.

This 1969 photo shows a U.S. lunar module on the far side of the moon.

Dr. Eugene Shoemaker of the U.S. Geological Survey, one of the principal investigators for the Surveyor project, puts it this way:

"The moon's face is certainly not a deep sea of very fine dust. Undoubtedly half the materials are finer than the smallest particles we can see in the Surveyor pictures, and we have measured and counted particles no bigger than a fiftieth of an inch. That is to say, it is like fine sand, or finer, in grain size. But distributed through this are many coarser particles. So it is a very gritty, silt-like material with blocks and chips throughout.

"It is relatively easily disturbed. The effects of the Surveyor footpads landing on its surface are not unlike the effects of walking across a freshly plowed field."

Dust Would Have Fooled Craft's Radar

How can we be so sure about the absence of loose dust? First, by looking at Surveyor's footprint. The robot's foot has sunk a little way down, just as it would in freshly cultivated soil or in wet beach sand.

Second, the very fact that Surveyor landed so well indicates that there could not be a thick bed of loose dust. Had there been, the landing signal would have penetrated deeply into the dust, and would have deceived the radar about the craft's altitude in the last moments before landing.

There is still another indication. No continuous layer of dust was observed by the television camera on any of the parts of the spacecraft. And obviously, no dust gathered on the camera lens, or our pictures would have been fogged and blurred.

To find out how much weight the lunar surface will support, Dr. Ronald Scott, a soil mechanics expert from the California Institute of Technology, experimented for many hours with a sandbox resembling those used in kindergartens. He varied lighting angles, trying to duplicate lighting effects seen in the moon pictures, to gauge the depth of penetration of the footpads and thus help interpret the properties of the lunar material.

Modules Safety Hinges on Landing Site

Dr. Scott and his colleagues concluded that if the surface material is uniform to a depth of at least a foot, it will support about five pounds to the square inch.

"A man walking on the surface would be in no danger of sinking," says Dr. Scott.

"This determination of the bearing strength of the moon's surface may indeed be the most important of Surveyor's discoveries," adds Benjamin Milwitzky, Surveyor Program Manager at NASA's headquarters.

But will the moon support Apollo's LEM, the Lunar Excursion Module, with its two astronauts? This craft will weigh 2,500 moon-pounds compared to Surveyor's skimpy 100; its landing system resembles Surveyor's.

Yes, we think LEM can land safely if it comes down properly and descends on a site like that on which Surveyor came to rest.

Nevertheless, Surveyor's pictures reveal serious hazards to any spacecraft in the many large rocks that litter even the smooth surfaces of the moon's plains. Dr. Elliot C. Morris of the U.S. Geological Survey estimates that in any area of a hundred square yards, one would expect to find at least one boulder two to three feet across, and many more smaller rocks or fragments.

"In some ways the surface of the moon is definitely more hostile than we thought it might be," says Dr. Robert L. Roderick, Surveyor Program Manager of Hughes Aircraft Company, where the spacecraft was built. "Judging from the Ranger pictures, we did not expect to find such large rocks or so many of them."

If a spacecraft hit [a] rock-strewn field . . . , it would not be likely to survive. So it is clear that the astronauts will need to maneuver the LEM to the type of landing spot Surveyor found.

Surveyor tells much about the moon besides the all-important question of its surface. Temperature sensors show what the astronauts may expect in the way of heat and cold. At lunar noon, with the sun's radiation pouring directly down, the moon surface reached 235° F., 23 degrees above the boiling point of water on earth. At sundown heat fled swiftly; the temperature plunged to zero within an hour, and then dropped to about –250° F.

Surveyors to come will add much more to our scientific knowledge. One may carry a scoop to dig a trench for observation of subsurface features to a depth of perhaps 18 inches. Plans call also for an instrument to ascertain the chemical elements in the lunar material; a seismometer to check for moonquakes, to help determine whether the moon is inert or is active internally; and dual cameras to take stereoscopic pictures.

The United States has put its first footprints on the moon. These were made by the aluminum-shod feet of a three-legged robot, to be sure, but they were necessary before man himself could walk there.

Black Power!

By Stokely Carmichael

On June 5, 1966, James Meredith began his March Against Fear in Memphis, Tennessee, intending to walk to Jackson, Mississippi, a distance of about two hundred miles. Meredith's admission to and integration of Ole Miss (the University of Mississippi) in 1962 had been marked by racial tension that often erupted in violence against African Americans in the South. Meredith's march was an attempt to prove to himself and others that African Americans should be able to safely move about in the Deep South without fear. Along the way, he also encouraged African Americans to vote. In Meredith's view, only by overcoming the fear of white intimidation in the community and at the polls could African Americans strike a crippling blow against oppression.

Soon after leaving Memphis, Meredith was shot by a sniper and hospitalized. Other civil rights leaders and workers, including Dr. Martin Luther King Jr. and Stokely Carmichael, heard the news and decided to continue the march in Meredith's name. Carmichael, chairman of the Student Nonviolent Coordinating Committee (SNCC) in 1966, was arrested during the march. He wrote and delivered his "Black Power" speech, excerpted below, after being released.

Carmichael's message was that years of nonviolent protest had achieved few political goals and done little to stop the wanton murder of African Americans. He now advocated that African Americans take pride in their culture and assume power over their own destinies instead of petitioning whites for necessary changes. Part of this "black power" was a declaration that African Americans should respond to white violence in kind. Carmichael's decision to abandon nonviolent rhetoric revealed a growing frustration in the black community with the slow progress of the civil rights movement.

Carmichael was born in 1941 in Trinidad and moved to the United States in 1952. He attended high school in New York City, and college at Howard University in Washington, D.C. By the end of the 1960s, Carmichael had completely lost faith in the U.S. ability to ensure racial equality. He moved to Guinea in West Africa to support and study under socialist politician Kwame Nkrumah. Out of respect for his mentor and his adopted culture, Carmichael changed his name to Kwame Ture. Ture continued to write and speak on behalf of socialism for decades until he died of prostate cancer in 1998.

T his is 1966 and it seems to me that it's "time out" for nice words. It's time black people got together. We have to say things nobody else in this country is willing to say and find the strength internally and from each other to say the things that need to be said. We have to understand the lies this country has spoken about black people and we have to set the record straight. No one else can do that but black people.

I remember when I was in school they used to say, "If you work real hard, if you sweat, if you are ambitious, then you will be successful." I'm here to tell you that if that was true, black people would own this country, because we sweat more than anybody else in this country. We have to say to this country that you have lied to us. We picked your cotton for $2.00 a day, we washed your dishes, we're the porters in your bank and in your building, we are the janitors and the elevator men. We worked hard and all we get is a little pay and a hard way to go from you. We have to talk not only about what's going on here but what this country is doing across the world. When we start getting the internal strength to tell them what should be told and to speak the truth as it should be spoken, let them pick the sides and let the chips fall where they may.

Don't Be Ashamed of Your Color

Now, about what black people have to do and what has been done to us by white people. If you are born in Lowndes County, Alabama, Swillingchit, Mississippi, or Harlem, New York, and the color of your skin happens to be black you are going to catch it. The only reason we have to get together is the color of our skins. They oppress us because we are black and we are going to use that blackness to get out of the trick bag they put us in. Don't be ashamed of your color.

A few years ago, white people used to say, "Well, the reason they live in the ghetto is they are stupid, dumb, lazy, unambitious, apathetic, don't care, happy, contented," and the trouble was a whole lot of us believed that junk about ourselves. We were so busy trying to prove to white folks that we were everything they said we weren't that we got so busy being white we forgot what it was to be black. We are going to call our black brother's hand.

Now, after 1960, when we got moving, they couldn't say we were lazy and dumb and apathetic and all that anymore so they got sophisticated and started to play the dozens with us. They called conferences about our mamas and told us that's why we were where we were at. Some people were sitting up there talking with [President Lyndon] Johnson while he was talking about their mamas. I don't play the dozens with white folks. To set the record straight, the reason we are in the bag we are in isn't because of my mama, it's because of what they did to my mama. That's why I'm where I'm at. We have to put the blame where it belongs. The blame does not belong on the oppressed but on the oppressor, and that's where it is going to stay.

Don't let them scare you when you start opening your mouth—speak the truth. Tell them, "Don't blame us because we haven't ever had the chance to do wrong." They made sure that we have been so blocked-in we couldn't move until they said, "Move." Now there are a number of things we have to do. The only thing we own in this country is the color of our skins and we are ashamed of that because they made us ashamed. We have to stop being ashamed of being black. A broad nose, a thick lip and nappy hair is us and we are going to call that beautiful whether they like it or not. We are not going to fry our hair anymore but they can start wearing their hair natural to look like us.

We Have to Define Ourselves

We have to define how we are going to move, not how they say we can move. We have never been able to do that before. Everybody in this country jumps up and says, "I'm a friend of the civil rights movement. I'm a friend of the Negro." We haven't had the chance to say whether or not that man is stabbing us in the back or not. All those people who are calling us friends are nothing but treacherous enemies and we can take care of our enemies but God deliver us from our "friends." The only protection we are going to have is from each other. We have to build a strong base to let them know if they touch one black man driving his wife to the hospital in Los Angeles, or one black man walking down a highway in Mississippi or if they take one black man who has a rebellion and put him in jail and start talking treason, we are going to disrupt this whole country.

We have to say, "Don't play jive and start writing poems after Malcolm [X] is shot." We have to move from the point where the man left off and stop writing poems. We have to start supporting our own movement. If we can spend all that money to send a preacher to a Baptist convention in a Cadillac then we can spend money to support our own movement.

Now let's get to what the white press has been calling riots. In the first place don't get confused with the words they use like "anti-white," "hate," "militant" and all that nonsense like "radical" and "riots." What's happening is rebellions not riots. . . . The extremists in this country are the white people who force us to live the way we live. We have to define our own ethic. We don't have to (and don't make any apologies about it) obey any law that we didn't have a part to make, especially if that law was made to keep us where we are. We have the right to break it.

We have to stop apologizing for each other. We must tell our

Stokely Carmichael, head of the Student Non-Violent Coordinating Committee, addresses a crowd of fourteen thousand people at Berkeley on October 29, 1966.

black brothers and sisters who go to college, "Don't take any job for IBM or Wall Street because you aren't doing anything for us. You are helping this country perpetuate its lies about how democracy rises in this country." They have to come back to the community, where they belong and use their skills to help develop us. We have to tell the doctors, "You can't go to college and come back and charge us $5.00 and $10.00 a visit. You have to charge us 50 cents and be thankful you get that." We have to tell our lawyers not to charge us what they charge but to be happy to take a case and plead it free of charge. We have to define success and tell them the food [African American diplomat and Nobel Peace Prize recipient] Ralph Bunche eats doesn't feed our hungry stomachs. We have to tell Ralph Bunche the only reason he is up there is so when we yell they can pull him out. We have to do that, nobody else can do that for us.

We have to talk about wars and soldiers and just what that means. A mercenary is a hired killer and any black man serving in this man's army is a black mercenary, nothing else. A mercenary fights for a country for a price but does not enjoy the rights of the country for which he is fighting. A mercenary will go to Vietnam to fight for free elections for the Vietnamese but doesn't have free elections in Alabama, Mississippi, Georgia, Texas, Louisiana, South Carolina and Washington, D.C. A mercenary goes to Vietnam and gets shot fighting for his country and they won't even bury him in his own hometown. He's a mercenary, that's all. We must find the strength so that when they start grabbing us to fight their war we say, "Hell no."

We have to talk about nonviolence among us, so that we don't cut each other on Friday nights and don't destroy each other but move to a point where we appreciate and love each other. That's the nonviolence that has to be talked about. The psychology the man has used on us has turned us against each other. He says nothing about the cutting that goes on Friday night but talk about raising one fingertip towards him and that's when he jumps up. We have to talk about nonviolence among us first.

Know Your Own History

We have to study black history but don't get fooled. You should know who John Hullett is, and Fannie Lou Hamer is, who Lerone Bennett is, who Max Stanford is, who Lawrence Landry is, who May Mallory is and who Robert Williams is. You have to know these people yourselves because you can't read about them in a book or in the press. You have to know what Mr. X said from his own lips not the *Chicago Sun-Times*. That responsibility is ours. The Muslims call themselves Muslims but the press calls them black Muslims. We have to call them Muslims and go to their mosque to find out what they are talking about firsthand and then we can talk about getting together. Don't let that man get up there and tell you, "Oh, you know those Muslims preach nothing but hate. You shouldn't be messing with them." "Yah, I don't mess with them, yah, I know they bad." The man's name is the Honorable Elijah Muhammad and he represents a great section of the black community. Honor him.

We have to go out and find our young blacks who are cutting and shooting each other and tell them they are doing the cutting and shooting to the wrong people. We have to bring them together and spend the time if we are not just shucking and jiving. This is 1966 and my grandmother used to tell me, "The time is far spent." We have to move this year.

There is a psychological war going on in this country and it's whether or not black people are going to be able to use the terms they want about their movement without white people's blessing. We have to tell them we are going to use the term "Black Power" and we are going to define it because Black Power speaks to us. We can't let them project Black Power because they can only project it from white power and we know what white power has done to us. We have to organize ourselves to speak from a position of strength and stop begging people to look kindly upon us. We are going to build a movement in this country based on the color of our skins that is going to free us from our oppressors and we have to do that ourselves.

We have got to understand what is going on in Lowndes County, Alabama, what it means, who is in it and what they are doing so if white people steal that election like they do all over this country then the eyes of black people all over this country will be focused there to let them know we are going to take care of business if they mess with us in Lowndes County. That responsibility lies on all of us, not just the civil rights workers and do-gooders.

If we talk about education we have to educate ourselves, not with Hegel or Plato or the missionaries who came to Africa with the Bible and we had the land and when they left we had the

Bible and they had the land. We have to tell them the only way anybody eliminates poverty in this country is to give poor people money. You don't have to Headstart, Uplift and Upward-Bound them into your culture. Just give us the money you stole from us, that's all. We have to say to people in this country, "We don't really care about you. For us to get better, we don't have to go to white things. We can do it in our own community, ourselves if you didn't steal the resources that belong there." We have to understand the Horatio Alger lie and that the individualist, profit-concept nonsense will never work for us. We have to form cooperatives and use the profits to benefit our community. We can't tolerate their system.

What Power Is

When we form coalitions we must say on what grounds we are going to form them, not white people telling us how to form them. We must build strength and pride amongst ourselves. We must think politically and get power because we are the only people in this country that are powerless. We are the only people who have to protect ourselves from our protectors. We are the only people who want a man called [Chicago school superintendent Benjamin C.] Willis removed who is a racist, that have to lie down in the street and beg a racist named [Chicago mayor Richard J.] Daley to remove the racist named Willis. We have to build a movement so we can see Daley and say, "Tell Willis to get hat," and by the time we turn around he is gone. That's Black Power.

Everybody in this country is for "Freedom Now" but not everybody is for Black Power because we have got to get rid of some of the people who have white power. We have got to get us some Black Power. We don't control anything but what white people say we can control. We have to be able to smash any political machine in the country that's oppressing us and bring it to its knees. We have to be aware that if we keep growing and multiplying the way we do in ten years all the major cities are going to be ours. We have to know that in Newark, New Jersey, where we are sixty percent of the population, we went along with their stories about integrating and we got absorbed. All we have to show for it is three councilmen who are speaking for them and not for us. We have to organize ourselves to speak for each other. That's Black Power. We have to move to control the economics and politics of our community.

The *Miranda* Ruling

By Liva Baker

"You have the right to remain silent. Anything you say can and will be held against you at trial. You have the right to an attorney. If you cannot afford an attorney, one will be appointed for you free of charge."

The Miranda warning, which police officers are required to read to anyone who is arrested, is a result of the U.S. Supreme Court's 1966 *Miranda v. Arizona* decision. Prior to this ruling, the Supreme Court had stated that confessions obtained during a private interrogation by police officers without a lawyer present were admissible as evidence.

In 1963, Ernesto Miranda was convicted of rape. The primary evidence against him was a confession he made during two hours of interrogation without his attorney present. His court-appointed attorney for that trial, Alvin Moore, had objected to the confession being allowed but in 1963, the accepted interpretation of constitutional law permitted prosecutors to use such confessions as evidence.

All of this changed with the *Miranda* ruling. Moore had appealed his client's case all the way to the Supreme Court, which overturned the original ruling. In his majority ruling, Chief Justice Earl Warren argued that the right to have an attorney present should be specifically protected before any confession is obtained.

The following is excerpted from journalist Liva Baker's 1983 book *Miranda: Crime, Law, and Politics*, in which she looks back on the *Miranda* decision.

The decision in Ernesto Miranda's and three . . . other confessions cases which had been argued together had been put together in the final decision as one case, under the umbrella of *Miranda v. Arizona.* It was one of seven full opinions handed down on Monday, June 13, 1966. Chief Justice Warren, his voice laden with emotion, read his entire opinion—which consumes sixty pages in the *United States Reports.* The reading required nearly an hour.

Once again the Court had divided along class lines, the justices born to families in humbler circumstances looking at the interrogation room through the eyes of the defendant, those born to families accustomed to privilege and influence looking at it through the eyes of the policeman. The former made up the majority [of Supreme Court justices]—[Earl] Warren, [Hugo] Black, [William O.] Douglas, and [William J.] Brennan [Jr.], plus the newest member of the Court, Abe Fortas—and there was something in the opinion for each justice. As another step in mankind's groping "for the proper scope of governmental power of the citizen," the decision rephrased Fortas's comments on the historical perspective at oral arguments. In its description of Ernesto Miranda as an "indigent Mexican defendant" and a "seriously disturbed individual". . . the decision addressed Mr. Justice Douglas's concern for a tendency of law enforcement to trade on "the weakness of individuals." In its application to "persons in *all* settings in which their freedom of action is curtailed in *any* significant way [italics added]," it attempted to address Mr. Justice Black's previous statement, at oral argument, that the Court need not determine when the prosecution began, that the Fifth Amendment had laid down an absolute rule against compulsory self-incrimination. And for Mr. Justice Brennan, self-appointed gadfly to state courts, the decision reaffirmed the applicability of the Fifth Amendment to practices and procedures there.

No one except the members of the Court knows whether the framework of the opinion was worked out among the members of the majority before the chief justice ever put pen to paper—a system relied on in the past—or whether Warren put the document together himself, his memory refreshed by the oral argument tapes. Remarkably, however, for an opinion that held such a high potential for public controversy, it had changed very little from the first draft circulated a month before. The rewriting of an early ambiguous reference to a lawyer's presence in the interrogation

room, the toning down of a derogatory comment on police practices, and some minor editing put the first draft in its final form,
its sweep remaining through all the drafts as broad as Anglo-
American legal history, its detail as minute as the rules of interrogation procedure. Whatever input the other justices had, the
opinion remained, too, a typical Warren opus. There were no ap-
parent legal mysteries to bewilder the uninitiated, no sophisms to
ensnare, no scholarly allusions or unfamiliar historical references
to clutter. Its lucidity was surpassed only by its high moral tone.

Although the United States Supreme Court had vacillated, hes-
itated, even sometimes reversed its direction during the three
decades since it had for the first time, in *Brown v. Mississippi*
(1936), reversed a conviction because a confession had been co-
erced, it had been headed all along toward this moment. Case by
tedious case, the standards for the taking of confessions and
statements of criminal suspects had been raised by the simple,
although inherently subjective, device of reversing convictions
when the circumstances of the taking had appeared to violate due
process of law. Now, the Court was attempting to remove the element of subjectivity from the judging of cases by grounding the
decision on the Fifth Amendment. It was also taking the un-
precedented step of imposing stringent rules on law enforcement
officers, rules that put restraints on their instincts and restrictions
on their zeal. In so doing, the Court was challenging the collec-
tive wisdom of police, prosecutors, the attorneys general of more
than half of the states, and a number of leading judges.

Warren was not two minutes into the reading of his opinion
before the crowd gathered in the courtroom got a good idea of
the direction in which the decision was headed.

The Ruling

"We start here," he declared . . . "with the premise that our holding is not an innovation in our jurisprudence, but is an application of principles long recognized and applied in other settings."
The direction was clear; only the distance the Court would travel
and the route remained unknown.

Shortly thereafter Warren spelled out the rules . . . :

[T]he prosecution may not use statements, whether exculpatory or
inculpatory, stemming from custodial interrogation of the defendant unless it demonstrates the use of procedural safeguards effec-

tive to secure the privileges against self-incrimination. By custodial interrogation, we mean questioning initiated by law enforcement officers after a person has been taken into custody or otherwise deprived of his freedom of action in any significant way. . . .

As for the procedural safeguards to be employed, unless other fully effective means are devised to inform accused persons of their rights of silence and to assure a continuous opportunity to exercise it, the following measures are required. Prior to any questioning, the person must be warned that he has a right to remain silent, that any statement he does make may be used as evidence against him, and that he has a right to the presence of an attorney, either retained or appointed. . . .

The defendant may waive effectuation of these rights, provided the waiver is made voluntarily, knowingly, and intelligently. If, however, he indicates in any manner and at any stage of the process that he wishes to consult with an attorney before speaking there can be no questioning. Likewise, if the individual is alone and indicates in any manner that he does not wish to be interrogated, the police may not question him. The mere fact that he may have answered some questions or volunteered some statements on his own does not deprive him of the right to refrain from answering any further inquiries until he has consulted with an attorney and thereafter consents to be questioned.

The remainder of Warren's opinion relied heavily for its philosophical underpinning on the amicus brief filed in behalf of the ACLU [American Civil Liberties Union]. Here, even the language was identical in parts.

First, Warren in the Court opinion went to some lengths to establish the need for protecting the accused during police interrogation by citing the psychological stratagems for obtaining confessions urged on police not by chiefs in the backwaters of America but by the most modern manual of instruction, whose authors, Fred Inbau and John Reid, were officers of the Chicago Police Scientific Crime Detection Laboratory, had had broad experience in writing for and lecturing to law enforcement authorities over two decades—and had warned, in the 1962 edition of their manual, that the U.S. Supreme Court might very well decide exactly what it was deciding today. Police rarely—although Warren cited an example or two—kicked and beat a suspect anymore.

Rather, they isolated him, played on his weaknesses, undermined his will to resist, and, when all else failed, resorted to trickery. Such an atmosphere, Warren declared, carried "its own badge of intimidation" just as "destructive of human dignity" as physical intimidation, and invoking the relevant provision of the Fifth Amendment to the U.S. Constitution, he swelled into his major theme: "The current practice of incommunicado interrogation is at odds with one of our Nation's most cherished principles—that the individual may not be compelled to incriminate himself."

Precedence

So that there would be no mistake about it, Warren went on to support his earlier statement that today's decision was not an innovation but only a contemporary application of long-recognized principles, not all American in origin. Indeed, he had found in a thirteenth-century commentary on the Book of Judges a biblical grounding for the Fifth Amendment to the U.S. Constitution— ". . . the principle that no man is to be declared guilty on his own admission is a divine decree." He described what was generally acknowledged to be the first known public appeal to an accused's right to silence, John Lilburne's eloquent refusal in 1637 to confess in the Court of Star Chamber to political crimes—"another fundamental right I then contended for, was, that no man's conscience ought to be racked by oaths imposed, to answer to questions concerning himself in matters criminal, or pretended to be so," as Lilburne himself had described the proceedings at his trial—after which Parliament had abolished that inquisitorial body. . . . Warren concluded: "Today, then, there can be no doubt that the Fifth Amendment privilege is available outside of criminal court proceedings and serves to protect persons in all settings in which their freedom of action is curtailed in any significant way from being compelled to incriminate themselves." Or, as Mr. Justice Black had declared in the last hour of oral argument:

> The Court held a long time ago that what that means is that the Government shall not compel a defendant to give evidence against himself anywhere or under any circumstances. So why do we have to determine when the prosecution actually begins? The words of the Amendment are very simple, and they've been construed as meaning that that means the Government mustn't compel a man to give evidence against himself anywhere, at any time.

To safeguard the Fifth Amendment right, however, Warren then departed from the ACLU brief which had pressed upon the justices the absolute necessity for the presence of a lawyer at all stages. The Court did not go that far. Suspects must be offered counsel, appointed if necessary, but they could also waive their rights and confess.

Perhaps anticipating the uproar that would follow announcement of *Miranda*, Warren acknowledged that "we cannot say that the Constitution necessarily requires adherence to any particular solution for the inherent compulsions of the interrogation process," and invited—indeed encouraged—Congress and the state legislatures to devise whatever methods they pleased to protect the rights of individuals. Unless and until, however, these institutions implemented "procedures which are at least as effective in apprising accused persons of their right of silence and in assuring a continuous opportunity to exercise it," the rules announced today must be followed.

Between the oral arguments and the decision this June day, Solicitor General [Thurgood] Marshall, at the request of the Court, had further described in a letter FBI practices regarding criminal suspects about which he had been questioned during the argument: The FBI had for two decades informed criminal suspects of their right to remain silent and to consult with their lawyers; after passage of the Criminal Justice Act of 1964, which provided free counsel for federal defendants unable to pay, the agents were required to inform suspects also of their right to free court-assigned counsel.

The Uniform Code of Military Justice, the English Judges' Rules, and the Evidence Ordinance of Ceylon, Warren declared in his opinion, made similar provisions. India and Scotland had laws on their books protecting criminal defendants at the interrogation stage of proceedings "without marked detrimental effect on criminal law enforcement." So, the implication was, could local American police.

Although this provision of the decision seemed to get lost in the passionate reactions that followed the Court's announcement of its decision, the spontaneous confession—the confession of "a person who enters a police station and states that he wishes to confess to a crime"—was *not* barred by the decision. The decision restricted only those confessions taken from an individual in custody. . . .

The Court reversed the judgment of the Arizona Supreme Court: "[I]t is clear that Miranda was not in any way apprised of his right to consult with an attorney and to have one present during the interrogation, nor was his right not to be compelled to incriminate himself effectively protected in any other manner. Without these warnings the statements were inadmissible.". . .

The suspense had ended. The Supreme Court of the United States had installed the Fifth Amendment to the Constitution, with the Sixth Amendment as watchdog, in the station houses of America. In a practical application, it had put police on notice that not only extreme behavior on their part—the beatings, the long detentions, the psychological manipulations—but also their routine behavior was under judicial surveillance. In the legal application, there was no longer any question of whether or not a suspect must retain or request counsel prior to interrogation by police; it was now the government's—state as well as federal—responsibility to offer it, furnish it if necessary, and assume the burden of proof if it was waived. In the social application, there was no longer any need for people with trouble to stand alone in front of the people with uniforms; the people with trouble now possessed the Constitution.

In its historical application, the Court opinion was a tacit acknowledgment of the broadening of judicial perspective from simple disapproval of police brutality three decades before to conferring constitutional rights and the wherewithal and opportunity to use them on all, rich and poor, guilty as well as innocent. It was thus far the highest achievement of civil libertarianism as translated into constitutional terms by the U.S. Supreme Court.

Richard Speck and the Chicago Slayings

By Paula Chin, Civia Tamarkin, Bonnie Bell, and Barbara Sandler

On July 13, 1966, Richard Speck committed what some describe as the crime of the century when he brutally murdered eight student nurses in Chicago. A school dropout, Speck had accumulated a sizable criminal record before he was twenty-one. Sought for questioning about other crimes, Speck moved to Chicago from Texas just a few months before the murders. After spending the day drinking at a bar on July 12, 1966, he went into an apartment building where several student nurses lived. Brandishing a gun, Speck overpowered his victims. He tied the ankles and wrists of nine young women, herded them into one bedroom, and told them that he would not hurt them. One by one, over the next five hours, he took eight of the women into a separate room and killed them. The ninth hid under a bed while Speck was slaying his eighth victim. Corazon Atienza thus escaped Speck's notice and his memory. After Speck left the building, Atienza was able to untie herself and report the tragedy. Within an hour, Chicago police began a search that would last for only a couple of days. The description provided by the surviving witness aided in identifying Speck, who ended up at a local hospital after a suicide attempt.

In 1991, Speck had a massive heart attack and died in prison. Freelance journalists Paula Chin, Civia Tamarkin, Bonnie Bell, and Barbara Sandler wrote this article shortly after his death to recount Speck's vicious crime.

Paula Chin, Civia Tamarkin, Bonnie Bell, and Barbara Sandler, "An Unfathomable Evil," *People Weekly*, vol. 36, December 23, 1991, p. 121. Copyright © 1991 by Time, Inc. Reproduced by permission.

The heat wave that had choked Chicago for nearly a week finally broke on the night of July 13, 1966, and inside the yellow-brick town house at 2319 East 100th Street, the residents were turning in for the night. Corazon Atienza, then a 23-year-old exchange nurse from the Philippines, still remembers locking the front door at 10:30, going upstairs to her small bedroom, then drifting off to sleep as her bunkmate said her prayers. And she recalls answering the four knocks on the bedroom door a half hour later, when the lanky young man with the pockmarked face and greasy, slicked-back hair pushed his way in. It was Richard Speck. "The first thing I noticed about him was the strong smell of alcohol," says Atienza, who was then known by her maiden name, Amurao. She also saw the small gun he had pulled from his black jacket.

As hard as she has tried, Atienza can never forget the horror of the next five hours as the killer who had come out of the darkness bound and then systematically stabbed, strangled and mutilated eight of her nursing school colleagues. Hiding under one bed after another, Atienza managed to survive—and to bear witness to a crime that ushered in the age of the mass murderer. Calculated and seemingly unmotivated, Speck's savagery evoked worldwide horror and headlines—and left a terrifying legacy: the gnawing fear that Americans weren't safe anymore, even in their own homes.

Profile of a Killer

On Dec. 5 [1991] a part of that terror ended when Speck, 49, died of a heart attack in a hospital near the Joliet, Ill., prison where he had been held for 24 years. "I feel relieved," says Atienza. "I prayed a lot. I've tried to live a normal life, but it's not been easy." Still, for her and the families of the dead, Speck's death cannot put to rest the anguished question—why did it happen? "He was the banality of evil," says William Martin, the attorney who prosecuted the case. "His whole life was a rehearsal for what he did the night of July 13, 1966." Speck was one of eight children born in Monmouth, Ill., to Mary Margaret Speck and her husband, Benjamin, a religious, hardworking potter who died when Richard was 6. After his mother married Texan Carl Lindberg in 1950, Richard and his younger sister, Carolyn, moved with the couple to Dallas. Even then he was troubled, a loner and a poor student who dropped out of school in ninth grade. His first arrest came at age 13, when he started a fire in a used-car lot. Over the next 11 years he was arrested 40 more times as he drifted from one odd job to another.

At 19, Speck married Shirley Malone, a 15-year-old he met at a county fair and with whom he had a daughter, Robbie Lynn, before he was sent to the state penitentiary at Huntsville, Texas, in 1963 for forgery and burglary. Released in 1965, he was divorced the following year and in March 1966 returned to Monmouth. By then the ex-con had a reputation as a knife-wielding, woman-abusing drinker and pill-popper who frequently got into barroom fights. The following month he went to Chicago, where he worked on and off as a seaman. After learning a job had fallen through on July 12, he spent most of the next day drinking at a bar before leaving around 10:30 P.M. and walking into the night.

The Murders

No one knows what Speck had in mind when he slipped in through the kitchen door of the town house and went to the second floor. At gunpoint he led Atienza and her bunkmate, 23-year-old Merlita Gargullo, to the large bedroom where four of their housemates—Valentina Pasion, 23, Nina Jo Schmale, 24, and Pamela Wilkening and Patricia Matusek, both 20—were sleeping. He ordered all six women to sit on the floor, telling them he only wanted money to go to New Orleans. After another student nurse, Gloria Jean Davy, 22, came into the room, Speck used his knife to slice a bedsheet into strips and began binding his victims' ankles and wrists. "Don't be afraid," he said, moving from woman to woman. "I'm not going to hurt you."

For a while he just sat there, smiling, smoking cigarettes and bantering. Then the killing orgy began. Speck untied Wilkening's ankles and marched her into another bedroom. Atienza heard a sigh, then silence; Wilkening was later found on the floor, gagged, strangled and stabbed in the left breast. When housemate Suzanne Farris, 21, and friend Mary Ann Jordan, 20, came into the bedroom, Speck appeared behind them and herded them into the room where he had taken Wilkening. There was a yell and brief sounds of a struggle. Some 20 minutes later came the sound of running water as Speck washed his hands after stabbing the two women 22 times.

The killings continued as Speck hauled his victims—some of them hiding under the bunk beds—from the floor and slaughtered them outside the room. His last victim was Davy, whom he raped on the bed while Atienza lay underneath a nearby bunk, silently praying. Then Speck took Davy to the living room and strangled her. Meantime, Atienza crawled under another bed where a blanket hanging to the floor concealed her. Speck returned to the room, shook Davy's purse to retrieve some change, and left. "I waited until I could hear nothing else in the house," Atienza recalls, "and I don't know how but I was able to untie myself." At 5:30 A.M. she walked to her bedroom and climbed out the window onto the ledge. "They are all dead! My friends are all dead!" she screamed. "Oh, God, I'm the only one alive!"

Speck on Trial

Within an hour, Atienza had described the murderer, and police fanned out in one of Chicago's largest dragnets. By the next day, detectives had matched up Speck's fingerprints from the town house with his arrest record and traced him to a North Side hotel. Speck had already left and checked into a skid-row flophouse, where the next night, apparently after learning he had left a survivor, Speck attempted suicide by slashing his wrists with a broken wine bottle. He was taken to Cook County Hospital, where an alert resident, Dr. Leroy Smith, recognized Speck from newspaper photos. Then, cleaning Speck's blood-caked arm, Smith uncovered the eerie tattoo saying BORN TO RAISE HELL that had been included in descriptions of Speck.

Nine months later a jury deliberated for only 49 minutes before convicting him of eight counts of murder. Speck stared coldly at them; he never flinched, even when he was sentenced to die in the electric chair. But in 1972, after the U.S. Supreme Court had reversed the death penalty in 41 cases—including Speck's—he was resentenced to eight consecutive terms of 50 to 150 years. It was a devastating blow to Atienza and to the victims' families, especially when Speck became eligible for parole in 1976. Whenever hearings were scheduled, relatives and friends of the slain nurses would make the pilgrimage to Statesville prison, and argue against his release. "It was heart-wrenching," says Marilyn McNulty, 47, Suzanne Farris's sister. "But we needed to keep the event alive, to say 'Don't forget' while there was still a breath in him. We couldn't forget. We can't ever forget."

Speck never did confess to his crimes, even after a quarter century in prison, where he collected stamps, painted in oils and made moonshine. When he died on Dec. 5, there was no mourn-ing—just relief, bitterness and regret. "It seemed like he died so easy," said Atienza, now a 48-year-old nurse at Georgetown University Hospital in Washington, D.C., and the married mother of two children, ages 20 and 22. "He should have died a long time ago." Cremated by the state, Speck took with him the horror of his crime. "The tragedy is we didn't learn a goddamn thing from Richard Speck, and his death seals his lips forever," says William Martin. "We'll never know why he did what he did."

The University of Texas Sniper

By David Nevin

Around noon on a hot August day at the University of Texas, an architectural engineering student named Charles Whitman armed himself with an arsenal of weapons and ammunition, went to the top of a 307-foot tower, and began shooting at people as they walked below. During the next hour and a half, he shot forty-five people, fifteen of whom died. His reign of terror ended when police stormed the tower and shot Whitman.

A few hours before going into the tower, Whitman murdered his wife and his mother. He then sat down and wrote a meticulous note describing what he was about to do. The thought of sitting on top of the Texas Tower and sniping at people had long been on his mind. For years, Whitman, an ex-marine, had casually mentioned to friends that the tower balcony would be a perfect site for a sniper. Four months before the shootings, he even mentioned his fantasy to a psychiatrist.

Best-selling author and journalist David Nevin was a staff writer for *Life Magazine* when he wrote this story in 1966. During the decade of the 1960s, he also covered other major stories for Time-Life News Services, including the assassination of John F. Kennedy, the civil rights movement, and the Cuban missile crisis.

Finally 90 minutes of indiscriminate slaughter came to an end. So did the life of Charles Whitman, gunned down by a policeman overcome by the monstrous event. When

David Nevin, "The Texas Sniper," *Life Magazine*, vol. 61, August 12, 1966, pp. 24–31. Copyright © 1966 by Time, Inc. Reproduced by permission.

Whitman dollied an arms-laden trunk across the lobby of the Administration Building, he had already killed his wife and mother.
Before he died he [had committed] the most savage one-man
rampage in the history of American crime.

What Whitman was doing was so outrageous, so hard to grasp,
that people could not believe it. Amid the spanging gunfire, students ambled to Chambers restaurant as on any other summer
day. Girls went on admiring the clothes in the windows of the
Co-Ed shop. Browsers at the University News glanced up, but
only briefly, from their books.

A boy and girl were killed in front of a bookstore. When a
group of gawkers gathered across the street Whitman struck
again, wounding three. A man died when he bent to help a preg-
nant woman—her child was stillborn.

A store manager was skeptical as three boys crawled in from
the sidewalk, moaning. "We're across the street from a big university," she said later, "and I wasn't about to fall for that. And
then I saw the blood—so much blood."

Charles J. Whitman was a man who carefully hid himself behind a sunny face of good nature and warmth. Scores of people
were fond of him, but probably only one really knew him well.
She was married to him, and she is dead.

When Whitman came down, very dead, from the tower on a
cart, his friends were incredulous. A slight, thoughtful boy named
Gary Boyd, who had shared classes with Whitman, said, "That's
not the Charlie Whitman I knew. When he got up there he was
somebody else. . . ."

Boyd was right. The Charlie Whitman he knew didn't exist.

All-American Boy

Boyd saw Whitman as "a real all-America boy." He was big,
strong, handsome, neat, hardworking. He was pleasant to be
around and interesting to talk with. He spoke ill of no one—except, occasionally, his father—and he tried to speak well of many
people. His grades were excellent. He enjoyed civic work, loved
his wife, admired his professors and seemed to have no enemies.

But he was also a violent man. He bit his nails to the quick and
perspired "rings of sweat on the coldest days." He was a meticulous perfectionist. He worked on engineering projects with passionate intensity but did not care for engineering or intend to remain in it. What he said in deep, intimate conversations seemed

to change from person to person.

There appears no question that, at the end, he hated his powerful, dominant father. Late one night he sat in the home of Barton D. Riley, an Austin architect and lecturer in the U.T. school of engineering. "If my father walked in that door right now," he said, "I would kill him."

"Charles," Riley said, "you don't mean that."

"I certainly do," said Whitman.

Yet at about this same time the elder Whitman came to Austin to visit. Charles introduced him to A.J. Vinicik, an Austin real estate man on whose recommendation Charles had become scoutmaster of a local troop. The two older men had a long, pleasant conversation and Vinicik was astounded to learn after the violence that Charles had disliked his father.

A Violent Young Man

Nor had Whitman always been the sunny, smiling lad his friends in the engineering school knew. Robert Ross, now a San Antonio businessman, recalls a poker game among friends in 1962 when he was a university sophomore. Whitman wore a 10-gallon hat. They played all night and at dawn Ross bet $190. Whitman called and lost. Whitman wrote a check for $190 and tossed it to Ross. The check bounced; the bank would only say that Whitman's account had been closed. Ross is 50 pounds lighter than Whitman and it was with trepidation that he called to demand his money. He found Whitman lying on a dormitory bunk in his underwear throwing a huge hunting knife into a closet door. Whitman grinned. "Look, kid," he said, "my family is loaded. I'll get you the money. Don't worry about it." The check was never made good.

That same year, 1962, Whitman married Kathleen Leissner, a pretty girl who was studying teaching. Kathy plainly loved him—but there is evidence she also feared him. He had joined the Marines in 1959 and was studying on an ROTC scholarship. His grades fell in 1963 and he returned to active duty to finish his hitch.

A young woman named Edith Molberg roomed with Kathy while Whitman was away, and she recalls that he beat his wife several times when he came home on leave. Kathy lived in terror of an accidental pregnancy, since Whitman had decided to delay children until he was through school.

Whitman was preoccupied with firearms. He had grown up in a household in which weapons were common, and he owned both pistols and rifles and was a good shot. Among the charges in his Marine court martial in late 1963—gambling, usury and threatening to kick out another Marine's teeth for failure to pay a debt—was the unauthorized possession of a small, unmilitary pistol. And at home, Kathy confided to her landlady that she was afraid to turn her husband's Luger over to the landlady for safe-keeping for fear "he'll beat me again." This pistol—purchased, according to Charlie's father, when he was a Marine at Guantánamo Bay—was part of his arsenal on the tower.

Whitman's best friend upon his return to school in January of 1965 was Larry Fuess, a muscular and handsome young architectural student with uncommon perception. Fuess knew that Charlie believed his father had beaten his mother. He also thought Charlie's chief fear was that he was inheriting his father's traits. A psychiatrist—to whom Whitman described two beatings given Kathy—thought the same thing.

Intensely Driven

In school again, Whitman's attitudes changed. He shifted from straight engineering to architectural engineering. His grades improved radically; so did his general attitude. And yet the pressures under which he purposely put himself seemed greater than ever.

He worked terribly hard. He carried 13 to 19 credit hours—15 hours is a normal full load. He also worked variously as a bank teller, a finance company collector and a clothing store salesman. Still his grades held up. Last fall he had nearly straight A's, and this spring he held a B average. Other students asked his help, which he gave graciously.

But to Whitman his best was never good enough. Barton Riley recalls a night when Whitman came to his house in despair because a project was not finished on time.

Another night, Whitman suddenly sat down at Riley's piano, and splendid music poured out for an hour and a half. Fuess was surprised when he heard of this. Riley hadn't known that Whitman refused to play for his friends.

None of his friends knew that Whitman was preparing to become a real estate broker. Despite his heavy schedule, he studied, took and passed the state licensing examination for real estate salesmen (at the time of his death he was a licensed and bonded salesman in the office of his friend from scouting, A.J. Vinicik—though he never sold anything).

During this period Whitman returned to scouting. He had been an Eagle Scout at 12, a considerable achievement, and now, as Vinicik put it, "He probably took up scouting just where he had left it as a boy. It was easy for him because he still was a boy." He took the boys camping, and on long hikes and nature trail studies. He taught them marksmanship in the careful, meticulous way of a man who knows and respects firearms. He used to hang a clothespin on a wire fence, start it spinning with .22 slugs and keep it spinning until the wood shattered. But after a few months he abandoned scouting.

Fuess recalls that Whitman was goaded by self-discipline, and that in turn he goaded Kathy. He set up a small gymnasium in his garage. "Wouldn't you think we would have enough self-discipline to exercise every day?" he would ask Kathy. Fuess and his pretty wife Elaine would look curiously at Whitman, for Kathy's figure was trim and neat and it was his own that troubled him.

Snap Decision

In March, Whitman's mother left his father and came to Austin to live. Whitman drove to Florida and brought her back. It seemed to disturb him deeply; he decided to quit school. Without telling even his wife, he resigned from college and sold his books and equipment. Fuess heard about this and went to Whitman's apartment to find him packing. Fuess asked him what he planned. Whitman thought he might travel the country, from city to city: "I don't know. I've just got to do it."

Whitman's faculty adviser, meanwhile, was alarmed. He called Whitman in, concluded that his troubles were largely financial and arranged a quasi-scholarship at Texas A&M. Whitman agreed. That afternoon he told Kathy he was leaving her. Later they went to the Fuess apartment, and Kathy kept asking, "But Charlie, why, why?" He couldn't answer. He shook his head.

Fuess noticed something that had been present all day: far from showing the agony of a man under great stress, Whitman was calm.

That night Fuess called Barton Riley. Riley is 41, muscular, an ex-Marine who was at Iwo Jima. He can be tough when he chooses. It was late but he called Whitman.

"This is ridiculous," he snapped. "You are not going to do it."

Riley told Whitman to skip the classes he had under Riley until he caught up in the others, then return and buckle down. Whitman said, "Yes sir." Within 10 minutes of Fuess's call to Riley, Whitman called Fuess and said, "I'll be there tomorrow." The next day Whitman saw Riley. He grinned. "Thank you, sir," he said.

His decision to leave had been made on the instant. His decision to stay was just as quick. Then, as if nothing had happened, he went on to recoup his class position and emerge with excellent grades. It left Fuess and Riley puzzled.

Kathy Whitman persuaded her husband to visit the university health center psychiatrist. Dr. M.D. Heatly immediately realized something that none of Whitman's friends suspected. "He readily admits," the psychiatrist wrote in a report, "having overwhelming periods of hostility. . . . Repeated inquiries attempting to analyze his exact experiences were not too successful with the exception of his vivid reference to 'thinking about going up on the tower with a deer rifle and start shooting people.'" The remark did not then alarm the doctor. Patients frequently make sweeping statements of general hostility. Heatly made an appointment for Whitman a week later. Whitman never came back.

Beginning of the End

On the Thursday before the deadly Monday, a student named Tom Brightman borrowed Whitman's classroom notes. Whitman was gracious, as usual, but told Brightman he needed to study them himself that night. The exchange indicates that on Thursday, Whitman was still a serious student.

But on Sunday evening, Larry and Elaine Fuess went by Whitman's home, as they frequently did, and he had changed. Kathy was at work and he was alone. When they came in his typewriter was set out and he said casually, "I was writing to a friend in Washington whom I haven't seen in five years." But the machine was empty and there was only blank paper beside it.

The Fuesses believe now that the deadly pattern had started and that they interrupted it and that he tolerated the interruption, perhaps even enjoyed it. They talked for about two hours, until 9:30 P.M., and Fuess noticed that Whitman was completely calm. He had stopped biting his nails. Fuess mentioned this and Whitman just grinned. There were two serious quizzes the next day and they talked briefly about them. Whitman said matter-of-factly that he didn't know the answers, had not covered the work and did not intend to take the quizzes.

Whitman was to pick up Kathy at 10 P.M. She had worked a split shift—in the morning and again at night in her summer job at the telephone company—and in the interval he had taken her to dinner and to a movie. It was obvious they had had a delightful time together. Twice Whitman began a sentence he did not finish. "It's a shame," he said, "that she should have to work all day and then come home to . . ."

They left and Whitman drove away to pick up Kathy. Within a few hours his mother, in her apartment, was dead, and in a few hours more, Kathy was dead.

The next afternoon, with the dead and wounded scattered like leaves on the ground, Larry Fuess crouched by a building and wondered, as did everyone else on the campus, who in God's name was up there. The name of Charlie Whitman flashed across his mind, and he was instantly ashamed that he could think such a thing of a friend. When it was over, Larry saw Charlie's body carried from the tower.

Evaluating Policy on Vietnam

By Robert McNamara

U.S. defense secretary Robert McNamara returned from Vietnam in the
fall of 1966 with new concerns. U.S. efforts to aid the South Vietnamese in their struggle against the Vietcong (South Vietnamese Communist guerrillas) and North Vietnamese troops had resulted in ever-
increasing numbers of U.S. combat troops being involved in the war in
Vietnam. Sustained U.S. bombing raids of North Vietnam, known as
Operation Rolling Thunder, had been occurring for more than a year,
and had not been effective in stopping North Vietnamese troops from
moving south. Most importantly, the death toll of U.S. troops was
mounting.

In the United States, citizens were becoming increasingly demon-
strative in their protests about U.S. involvement. The more combat
troops sent to Southeast Asia, the louder the protests became. In addition, issues of imperialism, racism, unscrupulous foreign policy, and
civil disobedience dogged the government's conduct of the war and
added to the growing furor in America.

McNamara's recommendations to President Lyndon Johnson in the
following memorandum dated October 14, 1966, departed radically
from his earlier support for escalating U.S. military involvement. Rather
than suggesting a further troop buildup, he suggested that the troop
buildup be reduced. He also advised the president to seek peaceful ap-
proaches to ending the conflict and to get U.S. troops out of the fight.

Robert McNamara was born in San Francisco, California, on June 9,

Robert McNamara, "Actions Recommended for Vietnam," *Memorandum for President Lyndon
B. Johnson*, October 14, 1966.

1916. After graduating from the University of California in 1937, he earned an MBA degree from Harvard. He then taught at Harvard and later became assistant professor of business administration there. He entered the air force, was awarded the Legion of Merit, and was promoted to lieutenant colonel. After his discharge, McNamara worked for the Ford Motor Company, becoming president of the company in 1960. He then served as secretary of defense under presidents John F. Kennedy and Johnson. Although, as such, the controversial McNamara was considered one of the architects of the Vietnam War in the 1960s, his view of the conflict became more pessimistic as the war progressed.

1. *Evaluation of the situation.* In the report of my last trip to Vietnam almost a year ago, I stated that the odds were about even that, even with the then-recommended deployments, we would be faced in early 1967 with a military stand-off at a much higher level of conflict and with "pacification" still stalled. I am a little less pessimistic now in one respect. We have done somewhat better militarily than I anticipated. We have by and large blunted the Communist military initiative— any military victory in South Vietnam the Viet Cong may have had in mind 18 months ago has been thwarted by our emergency deployments and actions. And our program of bombing the North has exacted a price.

My concern continues, however, in other respects. This is because I see no reasonable way to bring the war to an end soon. Enemy morale has not broken—he apparently has adjusted to our stopping his drive for military victory and has adopted a strategy of keeping us busy and waiting us out (a strategy of attriting our national will). He knows that we have not been, and he believes we probably will not be, able to translate our military successes into the "end products"—broken enemy morale and political achievements by the GVN [Government of (South) Vietnam].

The one thing demonstrably going for us in Vietnam over the past year has been the large number of enemy killed-in-action resulting from the big military operations. Allowing for possible exaggeration in reports, the enemy must be taking losses—deaths in and after battle—at the rate of more than 60,000 a year. The infiltration routes would seem to be one-way trails to death for the North Vietnamese. Yet there is no sign of an impending break in enemy morale and it appears that he can more than replace his losses by infiltration from North Vietnam and recruitment in South Vietnam.

Pacification is a bad disappointment. We have good grounds to be pleased by the recent elections, by [South Vietnamese prime minister Nguyen Cao] Ky's 16 months in power, and by the faint signs of development of national political institutions and of a legitimate civil government. But none of this has translated itself into political achievements at Province level or below. Pacification has if anything gone backward. As compared with two, or four, years ago, enemy full-time regional forces and part-time guerrilla forces are larger; attacks, terrorism and sabotage have increased in scope and intensity; more railroads are closed and highways cut; the rice crop expected to come to market is smaller; we control little, if any, more of the population; the VC political infrastructure thrives in most of the country, continuing to give the enemy his enormous intelligence advantage; full security exists nowhere (now even behind the U.S. Marines' lines and in Saigon); in the countryside, the enemy almost completely controls the night.

Nor has the ROLLING THUNDER program of bombing the North either significantly affected infiltration or cracked the morale of Hanoi. There is agreement in the intelligence community on these facts.

In essence, we find ourselves—from the point of view of the important war (for the complicity of the people)—no better, and if anything worse off. This important war must be fought and won by the Vietnamese themselves. We have known this from the beginning. But the discouraging truth is that, as was the case in 1961 and 1963 and 1965, we have not found the formula, the catalyst, for training and inspiring them into effective action.

A Revised Course of Action

2. Recommended actions. In such an unpromising state of affairs, what should we do? We must continue to press the enemy militarily; we must make demonstrable progress in pacification; at the same time, we must add a new ingredient forced on us by the facts. Specifically, we must improve our position by getting ourselves into a military posture that we credibly would maintain indefinitely—a posture that makes trying to "wait us out" less attractive. I recommend a five-pronged course of action to achieve those ends.

a. Stabilize U.S. force-levels in Vietnam. It is my judgment that, barring a dramatic change in the war, we should limit the increase in U.S. forces in SVN [South Vietnam] in 1967 to 70,000 men and we should level off at the total of 470,000 which such an increase would provide. It is my view that this is enough to punish the enemy at the large-unit operations level and to keep the enemy's main forces from interrupting pacification. I believe also that even many more than 470,000 would not kill the enemy off in such numbers as to break their morale so long as they think they can wait us out. It is possible that such a 40 percent increase over our present level of 325,000 will break the enemy's morale in the short term; but if it does not, we must, I believe, be prepared for and have underway a long-term program premised on more than breaking the morale of main force units. A stabilized U.S. force level would be part of such a long-term program. It would put us in a position where negotiations would be more likely to be productive, but if they were not we could pursue the all-important pacification task with proper attention and resources and without the spectre of apparently endless escalation of U.S. deployments.

b. Install a barrier. A portion of the 470,000 troops—perhaps 10,000 to 20,000—should be devoted to the construction and maintenance of an infiltration barrier. Such a barrier would lie near the 17th parallel—would run from the sea, across the neck of South Vietnam (choking off the new infiltration routes through the DMZ [demilitarized zone]) and across the trails in Laos. This interdiction system (at an approximate cost of $1 billion) would comprise to the east a ground barrier of fences, wire, sensors, artillery, aircraft and mobile troops; and to the west—mainly in Laos—an interdiction zone covered by air-laid mines and bombing attacks pinpointed by air-laid acoustic sensors.

The barrier may not be fully effective at first, but I believe that it can be effective in time and that even the threat of its becoming effective can substantially change to our advantage the character of the war. It would hinder enemy efforts, would permit more efficient use of the limited number of friendly troops, and would be persuasive evidence both that our sole aim is to protect the South from the North and that we intend to see the job through.

c. Stabilize the ROLLING THUNDER program against the North. Attack sorties in North Vietnam have risen from about 4,000 per month at the end of last year to 6,000 per month in the first quarter of this year and 12,000 per month at present. Most of our 50 percent increase of deployed attack-capable aircraft has been absorbed in the attacks on North Vietnam. In North Vietnam, almost 84,000 attack sorties have been flown (about 25 percent against fixed targets), 45 percent during the past seven months.

Despite these efforts, it now appears that the North Vietnamese–Laotian road network will remain adequate to meet the requirements of the Communist forces in South Vietnam—this is so even if its capacity could be reduced by one-third and if combat activities were to be doubled. North Vietnam's serious need for trucks, spare parts and petroleum probably can, despite air attacks, be met by imports. The petroleum requirement for trucks involved in the infiltration movement, for example, has not been enough to present significant supply problems, and the effects of the attacks on the petroleum distribution system, while they have not yet been fully assessed, are not expected to cripple the flow of essential supplies. Furthermore, it is clear that, to bomb the North sufficiently to make a radical impact upon Hanoi's political, economic and social structure, would require an effort which we could make but which would not be stomached either by our own people or by world opinion; and it would involve a serious risk of drawing us into open war with China.

The North Vietnamese Are Paying a Price

The North Vietnamese are paying a price. They have been forced to assign some 300,000 personnel to the lines of communication in order to maintain the critical flow of personnel and material to the South. Now that the lines of communication have been manned, however, it is doubtful that either a large increase or decrease in our interdiction sorties would substantially change the cost to the enemy of maintaining the roads, railroads, and waterways or affect whether they are operational. It follows that the marginal sorties—probably the marginal 1,000 or even 5,000 sorties—per month against the lines of communication no longer have a significant impact on the war.

When this marginal inutility of added sorties against North Vietnam and Laos is compared with the crew and aircraft losses implicit in the activity (four men and aircraft and $20 million per 1,000 sorties), I recommend, as a minimum, against increasing the level of bombing of North Vietnam and against increasing the intensity of operations by changing the areas or kinds of targets struck.

Under these conditions, the bombing program would continue the pressure and would remain available as a bargaining counter to get talks started (or to trade off in talks). But, as in the case of a stabilized level of U.S. ground forces, the stabilization of ROLLING THUNDER would remove the prospect of ever escalating bombing as a factor complicating our political posture and distracting from the main job of pacification in South Vietnam.

U.S. Marines search for North Vietnamese army bunkers.

At the proper time, . . . I believe we should consider terminating bombing in all of North Vietnam, or at least in the Northeast zones, for an indefinite period in connection with covert moves toward peace.

Revolutionary Development

d. Pursue a vigorous pacification program. As mentioned above, the pacification (Revolutionary Development) program has been and is thoroughly stalled. The large-unit operations war, which we know best how to fight and where we have had our successes, is largely irrelevant to pacification as long as we do not lose it. By and large, the people in rural areas believe that the GVN when it comes will not stay but that the VC will; that cooperations with the GVN will be punished by the VC; that the GVN is really indifferent to the people's welfare; that the low-level GVN are tools of the local rich; and that the GVN is ridden with corruption.

Success in pacification depends on the interrelated functions of providing physical security, destroying the VC apparatus, motivating the people to cooperate and establishing responsive local government. An obviously necessary but not sufficient requirement for success of the Revolutionary Development cadre and police is vigorously conducted and adequately prolonged clearing operations by military troops, who will "stay" in the area, who behave themselves decently and who show some respect for the people.

This elemental requirement of pacification has been missing.

In almost no contested area designated for pacification in recent years have ARVN [Army of the Republic of Vietnam] forces actually "cleared and stayed" to a point where cadre teams, if available, could have stayed overnight in hamlets and survived, let alone accomplish their mission. VC units of company and even battalion size remain in operation, and they are more than large enough to overrun anything the local security forces can put up.

Now that the threat of a Communist main-force military victory has been thwarted by our emergency efforts, we must allocate far more attention and a portion of the regular military forces (at least half of the ARVN and perhaps a portion of the U.S. forces) to the task of providing an active and permanent security screen behind which the Revolutionary Development teams and police can operate and behind which the political struggle with the VC infrastructure can take place.

Massaging the Heart

The U.S. cannot do this pacification security job for the Vietnamese. All we can do is "Massage the heart." For one reason, it is known that we do not intend to stay; if our efforts worked at all, it would merely postpone the eventual confrontation of the VC and GVN infrastructures. The GVN must do the job; and I am convinced that drastic reform is needed if the GVN is going to be able to do it.

The first essential reform is in the attitude of GVN officials. They are generally apathetic, and there is corruption high and low. Often appointments, promotions, and draft deferments must be bought; and kickbacks on salaries are common. Cadre at the bottom can be no better than the system above them.

The second needed reform is in the attitude and conduct of the ARVN. The image of the government cannot improve unless and until the ARVN improves markedly. They do not understand the importance (or respectability) of pacification nor the importance to pacification of proper, disciplined conduct. Promotions, assignments and awards are often not made on merit, but rather on the basis of having a diploma, friends or relatives, or because of bribery. The ARVN is weak in dedication, direction and discipline.

Not enough ARVN are devoted to area and population security, and when the ARVN does attempt to support pacification, their actions do not last long enough; their tactics are bad despite U.S. prodding (no aggressive small-unit saturation patrolling, hamlet searches, quick-reaction contact, or offensive night ambushes); they do not make good use of intelligence; and their leadership and discipline are bad.

Furthermore, it is my conviction that a part of the problem undoubtedly lies in bad management on the American as well as the GVN side. Here split responsibility—or "no responsibility"—has resulted in too little hard pressure on the GVN to do its job and no really solid or realistic planning with respect to the whole effort. We must deal with this management problem and deal with it effectively.

One solution would be to consolidate all U.S. activities which are primarily part of the civilian pacification program and all persons engaged in such activities, providing a clear assignment of responsibility and a unified command under a civilian relieved of all other duties. Under this approach, there would be a carefully delineated division of responsibility between the civilian-in-charge and an element of COMUSMACV under a senior officer, who would give the subject of planning for and providing hamlet security the highest priority in attention and resources. Success will depend on the men selected for the jobs on both sides (they must be among the highest rank and most competent administrators in the U.S. Government), on complete cooperation among the U.S. elements, and on the extent to which the South Vietnamese can be shocked out of their present pattern of behavior. The first work of this reorganized U.S. pacification organization should be to produce within 60 days a realistic and detailed plan for the coming year.

From the political and public-relations viewpoint, this solution is preferable—if it works. But we cannot tolerate continued failure. If it fails after a fair trial, the only alternative in my view is to place the entire pacification program—civilian and military—under General Westmoreland. This alternative would result in the establishment of a Deputy COMUSMACV for Pacification who would be in command of all pacification staffs in Saigon and of all pacification staffs and activities in the field; one person in each corps, province and district would be responsible for the U.S. effort.

(It should be noted that progress in pacification, more than anything else, will persuade the enemy to negotiate or withdraw.)

Credible Peace Gestures

e. Press for Negotiations. I am not optimistic that Hanoi or the VC will respond to peace overtures now (explaining my recommendations above that we get into a level-off posture for the long pull). The ends sought by the two sides appear to be irreconcilable and the relative power balance is not in their view unfavorable to them. But three things can be done, I believe, to increase the prospects:

(1) Take steps to increase the credibility of our peace gestures in the minds of the enemy. There is considerable evidence both in private statements by the Communists and in the reports of competent Western officials who have talked with them that charges of U.S. bad faith are not solely propagandistic, but reflect deeply held beliefs. Analyses of Communists' statements and actions indicate that they firmly believe that American leadership really does not want the fighting to stop, and, that we are intent on winning a military victory in Vietnam and on main-

taining our presence there through a puppet regime supported by U.S. military bases.

As a way of projective U.S. bona fides, I believe that we should consider two possibilities with respect to our bombing program against the North, to be undertaken, if at all, at a time very carefully selected with a view to maximizing the chances of influencing the enemy and world opinion and to minimizing the chances that failure would strengthen the hand of the "hawks" at home: First, without fanfare, conditions, or avowal, whether the stand-down was permanent or temporary, stop bombing all of North Vietnam. It is generally thought that Hanoi will not agree to negotiations until they can claim that the bombing has stopped unconditionally. We should see what develops, retaining freedom to resume the bombing if nothing useful was forthcoming.

Alternatively, we could shift the weight-of-effort away from "Zones 6A and 6B"—zones including Hanoi and Haiphong and areas north of those two cities to the Chinese border. This alternative has some attraction in that it provides the North Vietnamese a "face saver" if only problems of "face" are holding up Hanoi peace gestures; it would narrow the bombing down directly to the objectionable infiltration (supporting the logic of a stop-infiltration/full-pause deal); and it would reduce the international heat on the U.S. Here, too, bombing of the Northeast could be resumed at any time, or "spot" attacks could be made there from time to time to keep North Vietnam off balance and to require her to pay almost the full cost by maintaining her repair crews in place. The sorties diverted from Zones 6A and 6B could be concentrated on infiltration routes in Zones 1 and 2 (the southern end of North Vietnam, including the Mu Gia Pass), in Laos and in South Vietnam.

To the same end of improving our credibility, we should seek ways—through words and deeds—to make believable our intention to withdraw our forces once the North Vietnamese aggression against the South stops. In particular, we should avoid any implication that we will stay in South Vietnam with bases or to guarantee any particular outcome to a solely South Vietnamese struggle.

(2) Try to split the VC off from Hanoi. The intelligence estimate is that evidence is overwhelming that the North Vietnamese dominate and control the National Front and the Viet Cong. Nev-

ertheless, I think we should continue and enlarge efforts to contact the VC/NLF and to probe ways to split members or sections off the VC/NLF organization.

(3) Press contacts with North Vietnam, the Soviet Union and other parties who might contribute toward a settlement.

(4) Develop a realistic plan providing a role for the VC in negotiations, postwar life, and government of the nation. An amnesty offer and proposals for national reconciliation would be steps in the right direction and should be parts of the plan. It is important that this plan be one which will appear reasonable, if not at first to Hanoi and the VC, at least to world opinion.

"Success Is a Mere Possibility"

3. The prognosis. The prognosis is bad that the war can be brought to a satisfactory conclusion within the next two years. The large-unit operations probably will not do it; negotiations probably will not do it. *While we should continue to pursue both of these routes in trying for a solution in the short run, we should recognize that success from them is a mere possibility, not a probability.*

The solution lies in girding, openly, for a longer war and in taking actions immediately which will in 12 to 18 months give clear evidence that the continuing costs and risks to the American people are acceptably limited, that the formula for success has been found, and that the end of the war is merely a matter of time. All of my recommendations will contribute to this strategy, but the one most difficult to implement is perhaps the most important one—enlivening the pacification program. The odds are less than even for this task, if only because we have failed consistently since 1961 to make a dent in the problem. But, because the 1967 trend of pacification will, I believe, be the main talisman of ultimate U.S. success or failure in Vietnam, extraordinary imagination and effort should go into changing the stripes of that problem.

President Thieu and Prime Minister Ky are thinking along similar lines. They told me that they do not expect the Enemy to negotiate or to modify his program in less than two years. Rather, they expect that enemy to continue to expand and to increase his activity. They expressed agreement with us that the key to success is pacification and that so far pacification has failed. They agree that we need clarification of GVN and U.S. roles and that the bulk of the ARVN should be shifted to pacification. Ky will, between January and July 1967, shift all ARVN infantry divisions to that role. And he is giving Thang, a good Revolutionary Development director, added powers. Thieu and Ky see this as part of a two-year (1967–68) schedule, in which offensive operations against enemy main force units are continued, carried on primarily by the U.S. and other Free-World forces. At the end of the two-year period, they believe the enemy may be willing to negotiate or to retreat from his current course of action.

Note: Neither the Secretary of State nor the JCS [Joint Chiefs of Staff] have yet had an opportunity to express their views on this report. Mr. Katzenbach and I have discussed many of its main conclusions and recommendations—in general, but not in all particulars, it expresses his views as well as my own.

Star Trek Debuts

By Gene Roddenberry

When the television show *Star Trek* originally premiered on NBC on September 8, 1966, with the episode "The Man Trap," there was little reason to believe that it would be very successful. Science fiction television series had traditionally done well only when relying on a self-contained episode format (as *The Twilight Zone* and *The Outer Limits* had), and the complex mythology of *Star Trek* relied on viewers willing to pay attention to the characteristics of specific alien races and the working of starships as the series progressed. Dismissed by network executives as "too cerebral," the show was canceled after three seasons.

What NBC executives did not expect was a massive cult following of people who had grown accustomed to *Star Trek*'s universe and way of storytelling, and craved more. NBC attempted to capitalize on this fan base with a *Star Trek* cartoon series, but it soon became clear that fans preferred to see their humans and aliens in the flesh. The original *Star Trek* cast was brought in for *Star Trek: The Motion Picture* (1979), which launched a series of successful films and introduced new fans to the *Star Trek* universe. Since then, *Star Trek* has inspired five spinoff television shows, ten motion pictures, and hundreds of novels. After almost forty years, it remains popular—the most successful and long-running science fiction franchise ever created.

Star Trek was the brainchild of television writer Gene Roddenberry, who suggested the experimental series when it became clear that his crime drama *The Lieutenant* might be up for cancellation. In this 1965 series proposal, Roddenberry outlines the rough draft of what would become *Star Trek*. None of the original characters was preserved, ex-

Stephen E. Whitfield and Gene Roddenberry, *The Making of Star Trek*. New York: Ballantine, 1968. Copyright © 1968 by Stephen E. Whitfield. All rights reserved. Reproduced by permission of the Literary Estate of Stephen E. Whitfield.

actly—here, Mr. Spock is described as a red-blooded Martian rather
than a green-blooded Vulcan, and all of the other major characters are
given different names (Robert T. April rather than James T. Kirk,
"Bones" Boyce rather than "Bones" McCoy, and so forth)—but the
concept behind the series and the personalities behind several of its
most central characters are already clear.

STAR TREK
Created by
Gene Roddenberry

STAR TREK will be a television "first". . .
     A one-hour science-fiction series with *continuing char-
acters.*
Combining the most varied in drama-action-adventure
with complete production practicality.
And with almost limitless story potential.
STAR TREK is a new kind of television science fiction *with
all the advantages of an anthology, but none of the
limitations.* How? Astronomers express it this way:

$$Ff^2 (MgE) - C^1Ri^1 \times M = L/So$$

Or to put it in simpler terms:
     . . . The number of stars in the Universe is so infinite that if
only *one in a billion* is a sun with planets . . .
     . . . and if only *one in a billion* of all these planets is of Earth
size and composition . . .
     . . . the Universe would still contain approximately
2,800,000,000,000,000,000,000,000,000,000 planets capable of
supporting oxygen-carbon life . . .
     . . . or (by the most conservative estimates of chemical or or-
ganic probability) something like three million worlds with a
good possibility of intelligent life and social evolution similar to
our own.

The Series Pitch

Or to put STAR TREK into the language of television . . .
     THE FORMAT is "Wagon Train to the Stars"—built around char-
acters who travel to other worlds and meet the jeopardy and adventure which become our stories.

THE TIME could be 1995 or even 2995—close enough to our times for our continuing cast to be people like us, but far enough into the future for galaxy travel to be fully established.

THE FAMILIAR LOCALE is their vessel—the U.S.S. *Enterprise*, a naval cruiser-size spaceship. (In the initial draft of the format, the ship was the U.S.S. *Yorktown*.) The vessel (a permanent set) includes bridge, control rooms, crew quarters and facilities, science labs and technical departments, plus passenger and cargo accommodations. These compartments contain the wide range of personalities, some becoming Guest Star roles for stories aboard ship or on the worlds we visit.

THE LEAD ROLE is *Captain Robert T. April*, mid-thirties, an unusually strong and colorful personality, the commander of the cruiser.

OTHER CAST REGULARS are a variety of excitingly different types: *"Number One,"* a glacierlike, efficient female who serves as ship's Executive Officer; *José "Joe" Tyler*, the brilliant but sometimes immature Navigator; *Mr. Spock*, with a red-hued satanic look and surprisingly gentle manners; *Philip "Bones" Boyce*, M.D., ship's doctor and worldly cynic; and uncomfortably lovely *J.M. Colt*, the Captain's Yeoman.

The *Enterprise*'s Mission

The STAR TREK springboard to 3,000,000 worlds . . .

(Excerpted from orders to Captain Robert T. April)

III. You are therefore posted, effective immediately, to command the following: The U.S.S. *Enterprise*.
Cruiser Class—Gross 190,000 tons
Crew Complement—203 persons
Drive—space-warp
Range—18 years at light-year velocity
Registry—Earth, United Spaceship

IV. Nature and duration of mission:
Galaxy exploration and investigation;
5 years

V. You will patrol the Ninth Quadrant, beginning with Alpha Centauri and extending to the outer Pinial Galaxy limit.

VI. Consistent with the limitations of your vessel and equipment, you will confine your landings and contacts to Class "M" planets approximating Earth-Mars conditions.

VII. You will conduct this patrol to accomplish primarily:
   (a) Earth security, via exploration of intelligence and so-
       cial systems capable of a galaxial threat, and
   (b) Scientific investigation to add to the Earth's body of
       knowledge of alien life forms and social systems, and
   (c) Any required assistance to the several Earth colonies
       in this quadrant, and the enforcement of appropriate
       statutes affecting such Federated commerce vessels
       and traders as you may contact in the course of your
       mission.

The *Star Trek* Universe

The STAR TREK key is the bold establishing of . . .

GALAXY TRAVEL FULLY PERFECTED. April and his crew, unlike our limited astronauts of today, *are in charge of their own destiny, must find their own answers to the jeopardies they meet on far-off worlds.* The perfected spaceship concept allows us to move efficiently from story to story, freeing the audience from tiresome details of technology and hardware. Our aim is drama and adventure.

THE U.S.S. ENTERPRISE. A permanent set, also provides us with a familiar week-to-week locale. There is even a suggestion of current naval terminology and custom which helps link our own "today" with STAR TREK's "tomorrow." As with "Gunsmoke"'s Dodge City, "Kildare"'s Blair General Hospital, our Cruiser is a complete and highly varied community; we can, at any time, take our camera down a passageway and find a guest star (scientist, specialist, ordinary airman, passenger or stowaway) who can propel us into a new story.

THE SIMILAR WORLDS CONCEPT. Just as the laws of matter and energy makes probable the other planets of Earth composition and atmosphere, certain chemical and organic laws make equally probable wide evolution into humanlike creatures and civilizations with points of similarity to our own. All of which gives extraordinary story latitude—ranging from worlds which parallel our own yesterday, our present, to our breathtaking distant future.

STAR TREK *keeps all of Science Fiction's variety and excitement, but still stays within a mass audience frame of reference . . .*

By avoiding "way-out" fantasy and cerebral science theorem and instead concentrating on problem and peril met by our very human and very identifiable continuing characters.

Fully one-third of the most successful of all Science Fiction is in this "practical" category. Tales of exotic "methane atmosphere worlds with six-headed monsters" are rare among the Science Fiction classics. The best and most popular *feature highly dramatic variations on recognizable things and themes.* But even within these limits, there are myriad stories, both bizarre and shocking, plus a few monsters legitimus. Space is a place of infinite variety and danger.

Plot Points

Some other STAR TREK keys . . .

PLANET LANDINGS. The cruiser itself stays in space orbit, rarely lands upon a planet. Recon parties (small groups, featuring continuing characters) are set down via an energy-matter scrambler which can "materialize" them onto the planet's surface. This requires maximum beam power and is a tremendous drain on the cruiser's power supply. It can be done only across relatively short line-of-sight distances. Materials and supplies can also be moved in this same manner, but require a less critical power expenditure.

Landings are made for a wide variety of reasons—scheduled ports of call, resupplying the cruiser, aid to Earth colonies, scrutiny of an Earth commercial activity, collection of rare animal or plant specimens, a courtesy call on alien life contacted by earlier exploration, a survey of mineral deposits, or any combination of scientific, political, security, or supply needs.

Recon party landings always include dangerous unknowns— no amount of monitoring and observation from cruiser orbit can guarantee complete knowledge of all conditions down there. They can be attacked by alien life, totally ignored, and sometimes even find themselves forced to pose as members of a strange planet's society.

ALIEN LIFE. Normal production casting of much of this alien life is made practical by the SIMILAR WORLDS CONCEPT. To give continual variety, use will, of course, be made of wigs, skin coloration, changes in noses, hands, ears, and even the occasional addition of tails and such.

As exciting as physical differences, and often even more so, will be the universe's incredible differences in social organizations, customs, habit, nourishment, religion, sex, politics, morals, intellect, locomotion, family life, emotions, etc.

LANGUAGE. Simplified by the establishment of a "telecommunicator" device early in the series. Carried in a pocket, little more complicated than a small transistor radio, it is a "two-way scrambler" that appears to be converting all alien language into English and vice versa.

WEAPONRY. Equally basic and simplified. The cruiser is armed with Lasser (sic). Beams for self-protection. Crew side arms are rifles and pistols which can be adjusted to fire either simple bullets, explosive projectiles, or hypodermic pellets which stun or tranquilize.

And finally, the STAR TREK format allows production-budget practicality . . .

. . . by extensive use of a basic and amortized standing set (U.S.S. *Enterprise*) . . .

. . . plus amortization also of miniaturization (i.e., the cruiser in space or orbit) . . .

. . . permits through its "similar world concept" a wide use of existing studio sets, backlots, and local locations, plus unusually good use of in-stock costume, contemporary and historical . . .

. . . minimizes special effects and process by establishing simplified equipment and methods (stet weapons, no space suits, etc.).

Introducing the Characters

PRINCIPAL CHARACTER: *Robert T. April.* The "Skipper," about thirty-four, Academy graduate, rank of Captain. Clearly the leading man and central character. This role, built about an unusual combination of colorful strengths and flaws, is designated for an actor of top repute and ability. A shorthand sketch of Robert April might be: "A space-age Captain Horatio Hornblower," constantly on trial with himself, lean and capable both mentally and physically.

Captain April will be the focus of many stories—in still others he may lead us into the introduction of a guest star around whom that episode centers.

A strong, complex personality, he is capable of action and decision which can verge on the heroic—and at the same time lives a continual battle with the self-doubt and the loneliness of command.

As with such men in the past (Drake, Cook, Bougainville, and Scott), April's primary weakness is a predilection to action over administration, a temptation to take the greatest risks onto himself. But, unlike most early explorers, he has an almost compulsive compassion for the rights and plights of others, alien as well as human.

OTHER CONTINUING CHARACTERS: *The Executive Officer.* Never referred to as anything but "Number One," this officer is female. Almost mysteriously female, in fact—slim and dark in a Nile Valley way, age uncertain, one of those women who will always look the same between years twenty and fifty. An extraordinarily efficient space officer, "Number One" enjoys playing it expressionless, cool—is probably Robert April's superior in detailed knowledge of the equipment, departments, and personnel aboard the vessel. When Captain April leaves the craft, "Number One" moves up to Acting Commander.

The Navigator. José (Joe) Tyler, Boston astronomer father and Brazilian mother, is boyishly handsome, still very much in the process of maturing. An unusual combination, he has inherited his father's mathematical ability. José Tyler, in fact, is a phenomenally brilliant mathematician and space theorist. But he has also inherited his mother's Latin temperament, fights a perpetual and highly personalized battle with his instruments and calculators, suspecting that space—and probably God, too—are engaged in a giant conspiracy to make his professional and personal life as difficult and uncomfortable as possible. Joe (or José, depending on the other party) is young enough to be painfully aware of the historical repute of Latins as lovers—and is in danger of failing this challenge on a cosmic scale.

Ship's Doctor. Philip Boyce, M.D., is a highly unlikely space traveler. Well into his fifties, he's worldly, humorously cynical, makes it a point to thoroughly enjoy his own weaknesses. He's also engaged in a perpetual battle of ideas and ideals with José. Captain April's only real confidant, "Bones" Boyce considers himself the only realist aboard, measures each new landing in terms of the annoyances it will personally create for him.

The First Lieutenant. The Captain's right-hand man, the working-level commander of all the ship's functions—ranging from manning the bridge to supervising the lowliest scrub detail. His name is Mr. Spock. And the first view of him can be almost frightening—a face so heavy-lidded and satanic you might almost expect him to have a forked tail. Probably half Martian, he has a slightly reddish complexion and semi-pointed ears. But strangely—Mr. Spock's quiet temperament is in dramatic contrast to his satanic look. Of all the crew aboard, he is the nearest to Captain April's equal, physically, emotionally, and as a commander of men. His primary weakness is an almost catlike curiosity over anything the slightest "alien."

The Captain's Yeoman. Except for problems in naval parlance, J.M. Colt would be called a yeo-woman. With a strip-queen figure even a uniform cannot hide, Colt serves as Captain's secretary, reporter, bookkeeper—and with surprising efficiency. She undoubtedly dreams of serving Robert April with equal efficiency in more personal departments.

The Platform of the Black Panther Party

By Huey P. Newton and Bobby Seale

The Black Panther Party for Self-Defense was founded in October 1966 by young African American political activists Huey P. Newton and Bobby Seale. Seale, the organization's chairman, and Newton, the minister of defense, met while students at Merritt College in Oakland, California.

The Black Panthers were formed partly in response to police brutality in the black community, especially in reaction to the high number of deaths resulting from white officers shooting down African American crime suspects. To indicate that African Americans were no longer tolerant of repressive police policy, the Panthers patrolled the streets carrying licensed shotguns and pistols and wearing an identifiable black beret. The message behind the image was to suggest that they would fight back against further abuse. The Panthers also networked with groups from other ethnic and cultural backgrounds in an effort to speak to other forms of oppression.

The Black Panther Party was an aggressive and race-centered organization, in sharp contrast to nonviolent and multiethnic civil rights groups that held the most national influence at the time. Although the Panthers' violent image made them many enemies, including FBI director J. Edgar Hoover (who once described them as "the greatest threat to the internal security of the country"), many of their initiatives—such as the Free Breakfast for School Children Program and the

Huey P. Newton and Bobby Seale, "October 1966 Black Panther Party and Program," *The Black Panther*, November 23, 1967.

Sickle Cell Anemia Research Foundation—addressed community needs in a less confrontational way.

Most of the original Black Panthers drifted apart during the early seventies, partly due to FBI interference. Newton continued to campaign for civil rights until he was murdered in 1989; in 1993, the Huey P. Newton Foundation was created to preserve his memory and "empower all people, but especially urban youth, to be builders of a true global community." Bobby Seale remains an influential writer and speaker.

The following "10 Point Plan" outlined by Newton and Seale lists the Black Panther Party's goals.

W hat We Want
    What We Believe
    1. We want freedom. We want power to determine the destiny of our black community.

We believe that black people will not be free until we are able to determine our destiny.

2. We want full employment for our people.

We believe that the federal government is responsible and obligated to give every man employment or a guaranteed income. We believe that if the white American businessmen will not give full employment,then the means of production should be taken from the businessmen and placed in the community so that the people of the community can organize and employ all of its people and give a high standard of living.

3. We want an end to the robbery by the white man of our black community.

We believe that this racist government has robbed us and now we are demanding the overdue debt of forty acres and two mules. Forty acres and two mules was promised 100 years ago as restitution for slave labor and mass murder of black people. We will accept the payment as currency which will be distributed to our many communities. The Germans are now aiding the Jews in Israel for the genocide of the Jewish people. The Germans murdered six million Jews. The American racist has taken part in the slaughter of over twenty million black people; therefore, we feel that this is a modest demand that we make.

4. We want decent housing, fit for shelter of human beings.

We believe that if the white landlords will not give decent

housing to our black community, then the housing and the land should be made into cooperatives so that our community, with government aid, can build and make decent housing for its people.

5. We want education for our people that exposes the true nature of this decadent American society. We want education that teaches us our true history and our role in the present-day society.

We believe in an educational system that will give to our people a knowledge of self. If a man does not have knowledge of himself and his position in society and the world, then he has little chance to relate to anything else.

6. We want all black men to be exempt from military service.

We believe that black people should not be forced to fight in the military service to defend a racist government that does not protect us. We will not fight and kill other people of color in the world who, like black people, are being victimized by the white racist government of America. We will protect ourselves from the force and violence of the racist police and the racist military, by whatever means necessary.

7. We want an immediate end to police brutality and murder of black people.

We believe we can end police brutality in our black community by organizing black self-defense groups that are dedicated to defending our black community from racist police oppression and brutality. The Second Amendment to the Constitution of the United States gives a right to bear arms. We therefore believe that all black people should arm themselves for self defense.

8. We want freedom for all black men held in federal, state, county and city prisons and jails.

We believe that all black people should be released from the many jails and prisons because they have not received a fair and impartial trial.

9. We want all black people when brought to trial to be tried in court by a jury of their peer group or people from their black communities, as defined by the Constitution of the United States.

We believe that the courts should follow the United States Constitution so that black people will receive fair trials. The 14th Amendment of the U.S. Constitution gives a man a right to be tried by his peer group. A peer is a person from a similar economic, social, religious, geographical, environmental, historical and racial background. To do this the court will be forced to select a jury from the black community from which the black defendant came. We have been, and are being tried by all-white juries that have no understanding of the "average reasoning man" of the black community.

10. We want land, bread, housing, education, clothing, justice and peace. And as our major political objective, a United Nations–supervised plebiscite to be held throughout the black colony in which only black colonial subjects will be allowed to participate for the purpose of determining the will of black people as to their national destiny.

When in the course of human events, it becomes necessary for one people to dissolve the political bands which have connected them with another, and to assume, among the powers of the earth, the separate and equal station to which the laws of nature and nature's God entitle them, a decent respect to the opinions of mankind requires that they should declare the causes which impel them to the separation.

We hold these truths to be self evident, that all men are created equal; that they are endowed by their Creator with certain unalienable rights; that among these are life, liberty, and the pursuit of happiness. That, to secure these rights, governments are instituted among men, deriving their just powers from the consent of the governed; that, whenever any form of government becomes destructive of these ends, it is the right of the people to alter or to abolish it, and to institute a new government, laying its foundation on such principles, and organizing its powers in such form, as to them shall seem most likely to effect their safety and happiness. Prudence, indeed, will dictate that governments long established should not be changed for light and transient causes; and accordingly, all experience hath shown, that mankind is more disposed to suffer, while evils are sufferable, than to right themselves by abolishing the forms to which they are accustomed. But, when a long train of abuses and usurpations, pursuing invariably the same object, evinces a design to reduce them under absolute despotism, it is their right, it is their duty, to throw off such government, and to provide new guards for their future security.

The National Organization for Women Is Formed

By the National Organization for Women

President John F. Kennedy established the President's Commission on the Status of Women in 1961. Its function was to determine whether females received unequal treatment in employment, education, politics, or otherwise. In 1963 that committee submitted its final report, documenting widespread discrimination against women. As a result of these findings, President Kennedy signed an executive order creating both the Citizen's Advisory Council on the Status of Women and the Interdepartmental Committee on the Status of Women. A year later, the Civil Rights Act of 1964 included a section known as Title VII, that prohibited employment discrimination based on race, color, religion, gender, or national origin. The Equal Employment Opportunity Commission (EEOC) was established for the purpose of implementing Title VII.

After the June 1966 meeting of the Third Annual Conference of Commissions on the Status of Women in Washington, D.C., some women felt that the EEOC had failed to enforce Title VII, thereby allowing gender discrimination to continue to exist. Their frustration resulted in the formation of the National Organization for Women (NOW), a separate organization dedicated to achieving full equality for all women by fighting discrimination and lobbying lawmakers. On October 29, 1966, the National Organization for Women adopted the following *Statement of Purpose*.

We, men and women who hereby constitute ourselves as the National Organization for Women, believe that the time has come for a new movement toward true equality for all women in America, and toward a fully equal partnership of the sexes, as part of the world-wide revolution of human rights now taking place within and beyond our national borders.

The purpose of NOW is to take action to bring women into full participation in the mainstream of American society now, exercising all the privileges and responsibilities thereof in truly equal partnership with men.

Our Purpose

We believe the time has come to move beyond the abstract argument, discussion and symposia over the status and special nature of women which has raged in America in recent years; the time has come to confront, with concrete action, the conditions that now prevent women from enjoying the equality of opportunity and freedom of choice which is their right as individual Americans, and as human beings.

NOW is dedicated to the proposition that women first and foremost are human beings, who, like all other people in our society, must have the chance to develop their fullest human potential. We believe that women can achieve such equality only by accepting to the full the challenges and responsibilities they share with all other people in our society, as part of the decision-making mainstream of American political, economic and social life.

We organize to initiate or support action, nationally or in any part of this nation, by individuals or organizations, to break through the silken curtain of prejudice and discrimination against women in government, industry, the professions, the churches, the political parties, the judiciary, the labor unions, in education, science, medicine, law, religion and every other field of importance in American society.

Enormous changes taking place in our society make it both possible and urgently necessary to advance the unfinished revolution of women toward true equality, now. With a life span lengthened to nearly seventy-five years, it is no longer either necessary or possible for women to devote the greater part of their lives to childbearing; yet childbearing and rearing—which continues to be a most important part of most women's lives—is still used to justify barring women from equal professional and economic participation and advance.

Today's technology has reduced most of the productive chores which women once performed in the home and in mass production industries based upon routine unskilled labor. This same technology has virtually eliminated the quality of muscular strength as a criterion for filling most jobs, while intensifying American industry's need for creative intelligence. In view of this new industrial revolution created by automation in the mid–twentieth century, women can and must participate in old and new fields of society in full equality—or become permanent outsiders.

Women's Status in Decline

Despite all the talk about the status of American women in recent years, the actual position of women in the United States has declined, and is declining, to an alarming degree throughout the 1950's and 1960's. Although 46.4 percent of all American women between the ages of eighteen and sixty-five now work outside the home, the overwhelming majority—75 percent—are in routine clerical, sales, or factory jobs, or they are household workers, cleaning women, hospital attendants. About two-thirds of Negro women workers are in the lowest paid service occupations. Working women are becoming increasingly—not less—concentrated on the bottom of the job ladder. As a consequence, full-time women workers today earn on the average only 60 percent of what men earn, and that wage gap has been increasing over the past twenty-five years in every major industry group. In 1964, of all women with a yearly income, 89 percent earned under $5,000 a year; half of all full-time year-round women workers earned less than $3,690; only 1.4 percent of full-time year-round women workers had an annual income of $10,000 or more.

Further, with higher education increasingly essential in today's [1966] society, too few women are entering and finishing college or going on to graduate or professional school. Today [as of 1966] women earn only one in three of the B.A.'s and M.A.'s granted, and one in ten of the Ph.D.'s.

In all the professions considered of importance to society, and in the executive ranks of industry and government, women are losing ground. Where they are present it is only a token handful. Women comprise less than 1 percent of federal judges; less than 4 percent of all lawyers; 7 percent of doctors. Yet women represent 53 percent of the U.S. population. And increasingly men are replacing women in the top positions in secondary and elementary schools, in social work, and in libraries—once thought to be women's fields.

Official pronouncements of the advance in the status of women hide not only the reality of this dangerous decline, but the fact that nothing is being done to stop it. The excellent reports of the President's Commission on the Status of Women and of the state commissions have not been fully implemented. Such commissions have power only to advise. They have no power to enforce their recommendations, nor have they the freedom to organize American women and men to press for action on them.

Betty Friedan, president of the National Organization for Women, addresses reporters in Washington, D.C. Minutes after this picture was taken, her sign was confiscated by police

The reports of these commissions have, however, created a basis upon which it is now possible to build.

Discrimination in employment on the basis of sex is now prohibited by federal law, in Title VII of the Civil Rights Act of 1964. But although nearly one-third of the cases brought before the Equal Employment Opportunity Commission during the first year dealt with sex discrimination and the proportion is increasing dramatically, the commission has not made clear its intention to enforce the law with the same seriousness on behalf of women as of other victims of discrimination. Many of these cases were Negro women, who are the victims of the double discrimination of race and sex. Until now, too few women's organizations and official spokesmen have been willing to speak out against these dangers facing women. Too many women have been restrained by the fear of being called "feminist."

There is no civil rights movement to speak for women, as there has been for Negroes and other victims of discrimination. The National Organization for Women must therefore begin to speak.

What Must Be Done

WE BELIEVE that the power of American law, and the protection guaranteed by the U.S. Constitution to the civil rights of all individuals, must be effectively applied and enforced to isolate and remove patterns of sex discrimination, to ensure equality of opportunity in employment and education, and equality of civil and political rights and responsibilities on behalf of women, as well as for Negroes and other deprived groups.

We realize that women's problems are linked to many broader questions of social justice; their solution will require concerted action by many groups. Therefore, convinced that human rights for all are indivisible, we expect to give active support to the common cause of equal rights for all those who suffer discrimination and deprivation, and we call upon other organizations committed to such goals to support our efforts toward equality for women.

WE DO NOT ACCEPT the token appointment of a few women to high-level positions in government and industry as a substitute for a serious continuing effort to recruit and advance women according to their individual abilities. To this end, we urge American government and industry to mobilize the same resources of ingenuity and command with which they have solved problems of far greater difficulty than those now impeding the progress of women.

WE BELIEVE that this nation has a capacity at least as great as other nations, to innovate new social institutions which will enable women to enjoy true equality of opportunity and responsibility in society, without conflict with their responsibilities as mothers and homemakers. In such innovations, America does not lead the Western world, but lags by decades behind many European countries. We do not accept the traditional assumption that a woman has to choose between marriage and motherhood, on the one hand, and serious participation in industry or the professions on the other. We question the present expectation that all normal women will retire from job or profession for ten or fifteen years, to devote their full time to raising children, only to reenter the job market at a relatively minor level. This in itself is a deterrent to the aspirations of women, to their acceptance into management or professional training courses, and to the very possibility of equality of opportunity or real choice, for all but a few women. Above all, we reject the assumption that these problems are the unique responsibility of each individual woman, rather than a basic social dilemma which society must solve. True equality of opportunity and freedom of choice for women requires such practical and possible innovations as a nationwide network of child-care centers, which will make it unnecessary for women to retire completely from society until their children are grown, and national programs to provide retraining for women who have chosen to care for their own children full time.

WE BELIEVE that it is as essential for every girl to be educated to her full potential of human ability as it is for every boy— with the knowledge that such education is the key to effective participation in today's economy and that, for a girl as for boy, education can only be serious where there is expectation that it will be used in society. We believe that American educators are capable of devising means of imparting such expectations to girl students. Moreover, we consider the decline in the proportion of women receiving higher and professional education to be evidence of discrimination. This discrimination may take the form of quotas against the admission of women to colleges and professional schools; lack of encouragement by parents, counselors and educators; denial of loans or fellowships; or the traditional or arbitrary procedures in graduate and professional training geared in terms of men, which inadvertently discriminate against women. We believe that the same serious attention must be given to high school dropouts who are girls as to boys.

A Call to Action

WE REJECT the current assumptions that a man must carry the sole burden of supporting himself, his wife, and family, and that a woman is automatically entitled to lifelong support by a man upon her marriage, or that marriage, home and family are primarily woman's world and responsibility—hers, to dominate, his to support. We believe that a true partnership between the sexes demands a different concept of marriage, an equitable sharing of the responsibilities of home and children and of the economic burdens of their support. We believe that proper recognition should be given to the economic and social value of homemaking and child care. To these ends, we will seek to open a reexamination of laws and mores governing marriage and divorce, for we believe that the current state of "half-equality" between the sexes discriminates against both men and women, and is the cause of much unnecessary hostility between the sexes.

WE BELIEVE that women must now exercise their political rights and responsibilities as American citizens. They must refuse to be segregated on the basis of sex into separate-and-not-equal ladies' auxiliaries in the political parties, and they must demand representation according to their numbers in the regularly constituted party committees—at local, state, and national levels—and in the informal power structure, participating fully in the selection of selection of candidates and political decision-making, and running for office themselves.

IN THE INTERESTS OF THE HUMAN DIGNITY OF WOMEN, we will protest and endeavor to change the false image of women now prevalent in the mass media, and in the texts, ceremonies, laws, and practices of our major social institutions. Such images perpetuate contempt for women by society and by women for themselves. We are similarly opposed to all policies and practices—in church, state, college, factory, or office—which, in the guise of protectiveness, not only deny opportunities but also foster in women self-denigration, dependence, and evasion of responsibility, undermine their confidence in their own abilities and foster contempt for women.

NOW WILL HOLD ITSELF INDEPENDENT OF ANY PO-

LITICAL PARTY in order to mobilize the political power of all women and men intent on our goals. We will strive to ensure that no party, candidate, President, senator, governor, congressman, or any public official who betrays or ignores the principle of full equality between the sexes is elected or appointed to office. If it is necessary to mobilize the votes of men and women who believe in our cause, in order to win for women the final right to be fully free and equal human beings, we so commit ourselves.

WE BELIEVE THAT women will do most to create a new image of women by *acting* now, and by speaking out in behalf of their own equality, freedom, and human dignity—not in pleas for special privilege, nor in enmity toward men, who are also victims of the current half-equality between the sexes—but in an active, self-respecting partnership with men. By so doing, women will develop confidence in their own ability to determine actively, in partnership with men, the conditions of their life, their choices, their future and their society.

Vietnam Draftees Flee to Canada

By *U.S. News & World Report*

As the Vietnam War escalated during 1966, the number of draft calls increased from fewer than ten thousand per month to more than thirty thousand per month. Meanwhile, U.S. military casualties increased and the possibility of victory in Vietnam began to seem more remote. The combination of these factors led many young people to seek asylum from U.S. draft laws in Canada, which had porous borders with the United States and an extradition treaty that did not include draft laws. A U.S. draftee escaping to Canada could avoid military service indefinitely. This option became a social movement in 1966, when an estimated one thousand U.S. civilians fled to Canada to avoid serving in the U.S. military. By the end of 1967, the number had increased to over twenty thousand.

This article from a 1966 issue of *U.S. News & World Report* highlights what was at the time a new strategy for those who sought to avoid the Vietnam draft.

Scores of young Americans, seeking to avoid military service, are finding a haven and help now in Canada.

A small but growing number of these youths are crossing the border from the U.S. as tourists, then settling down out of reach of either Selective Service or the FBI.

Once across the border, they cannot be extradited as evaders of the U.S. draft.

Canada's Acting Prime Minister, Paul Martin, said at a press conference in Ottawa September 15 that no query from the U.S. in connection with draft dodgers had been brought to the attention of the Canadian Government. He added:

"We do not feel under any obligation to enforce the laws in that regard of any other country."

In Quebec, one student organization advertises that it is setting up an "underground railway" to help American students get into Canada, along with machinery to aid them in enrolling in Canadian universities.

Another organization, based in Toronto, the Student Union for Peace Action, publishes a booklet of instructions for U.S. college students on how to get permanent-resident status in Canada. The booklet is aimed chiefly at graduating seniors.

Aid to Dodgers

Several pacifist and religious organizations, including the Canadian Friends Service Committee, a Quaker group, offer aid to draft dodgers who find themselves in Canada without jobs or money.

Most of these organizations are centered in Montreal, Toronto and Vancouver. There are offers to provide legal advice and assistance, to arrange for temporary housing and to provide job leads to U.S. youths who flee to Canada to escape the clutches of their draft boards.

How many of these draft evaders from the United States are now in Canada is not clear. Spokesmen for some of the "peace" organizations in Toronto report that as many as 300 to 400 American youths of draft age are in the Toronto area alone, and that there are now similar numbers in other city areas.

Officials of the Canadian immigration service in Ottawa refuse to give any estimates, but say stories about draft dodgers are "overblown."

Army of Unscrubbed

It is conceded by these officials that there is a steady flow of young drifters—of the long-haired, bearded, beatnik variety—moving from city to city in Canada now. Many are U.S. citizens who hide their identity by melting into the jungle of Canada's own unscrubbed youth.

Yet there is also reported to be a substantial return flow to the

Students protest the Vietnam draft.

United States of youths who spend a period of hesitation in Canada, then return to face their draft boards and "get square with Uncle Sam."

Canada is an easy country for an American to enter. One self-admitted draft dodger explains how he did it, in this way:

"It wasn't any problem. They didn't check me. They asked how long I would be staying and I said I wasn't sure—so they gave me a two-month visa."

No passports are required. No written visa is issued to an American who says he is entering for a vacation, or to fish, or on business. No names are taken for an ordinary border crossing. Only a head count is made at ports of entry on the Canadian-U.S. border.

In the case of people moving to Canada for a permanent change of residence, Canadian law requires that they present proof of good health, including a chest X ray, along with proof of sponsorship, an awaiting job, or money enough to live on.

It Is Easy to Switch

But in practice, many people enter Canada from the United States as visitors and switch to "landed immigrant" status later. This can be done with relative ease.

The booklet published by the Student Union for Peace Action

outlines these immigration rules, and points out that an American who enters Canada as a visitor and chooses to stay need have "little fear" of being returned to the U.S.

Inquiries concerning this booklet, according to a SUPA staff member, are coming from all parts of the United States, "with a few more from the Northern States." In Montreal, inquiries received by the Quebec Union of Students, which is advertising aid to draft-evading students, are reported to be up sharply.

Youths making inquiries from the United States have been classified by Anthony Hyde of SUPA, in a recent, copyrighted article in "The Detroit News," like this:

"The first are pacifists or conscientious objectors. Many of the people are religious objectors.

"The second category, which is by far the largest, are just ordinary Americans from middle-class backgrounds, who don't want to take the two years out of their lives.

"Then there is the third category, which is once again small, which is composed of people opposed to the war in Vietnam."

Help, but No Encouragement

Quakers of the Canadian Friends Service Committee concentrate their assistance on draft evaders already in Canada. David Newlands, general secretary of the committee, says: "We will not encourage them, but if they do come, we will help them."

The Friends Committee also is getting co-operation from the Fellowship of Reconciliation of Canada, a religious pacifist organization founded in England after World War I.

An official of still another church-affiliated group, the Central Committee for Conscientious Objectors, based in Philadelphia, reportedly has met with religious and student groups in Toronto in an effort to round up financial and job aid for American conscientious objectors in Canada.

Canada: Draft Free

Canada has no draft of its own, at this stage. Draft evasion is not an extraditable offense under international treaties between Canada and the U.S.

And Canadian immigration authorities say a man's motive for seeking landed-immigrant status in Canada is not subject to question.

"We don't press such questions as whether he is running away from debts or a bad domestic situation," says R.B. Curry, of the Ministry of Citizenship. "But of course if a man has a police record, or has been charged with a crime and is avoiding arrest, police reports would be available to us."

Draft dodgers, according to Mr. Curry, have not yet become a major problem, "and we think reports about them have been exaggerated."

An effort is being made now by the Canadian Immigration Department, however, to clamp down on the numbers of people who enter Canada as visitors and stay on in the country to get landed-immigrant status.

In July, Citizenship Minister Jean Marchand reported to the Canadian Parliament that there were nearly 20,000 applications for such status on hand, filed by people, many of them from the United States, who were already in Canada as visitors.

In addition, he estimated that there were 20,000 more in the country on a long-term basis who had not applied for immigrant status.

Rules then were eased to allow all such "illegal visitors" who could meet the normal immigrant qualifications to obtain permanent status—with a July 25 deadline.

Since July 25, immigration authorities insist that a closer watch has been kept on arriving visitors and rules regarding length of stay have been more rigidly enforced.

There are special rules for students, however, that make their admission easier on a long-term basis.

FBI agents stationed in Canada reportedly keep track of those American youths who are known to have violated the draft law, and are thus fugitives from U.S. justice.

Several cases have been reported of FBI agents' questioning non-Americans who had registered for the draft while living in the United States and then returned to Canada before being called. Some of these have stirred angry protests from political groups and in Canadian newspapers.

Co-operation at Borders

There is known to be close co-operation between the FBI and the Royal Canadian Mounted Police on all cross-border problems. Officials at RCMP headquarters in Ottawa are reluctant to talk about the extent of draft dodging, and will only state that there is "good co-operation" between the police forces of the two countries.

One recent case that stirred some protests involved the questioning of an admitted draft dodger, Tom Hathaway, by an RCMP constable on behalf of the FBI.

Canada's biggest magazine, the biweekly "Macleans," sharply condemned the "mounties" in an editorial titled: "Draft Dodgers Are Refugees, Not Criminals."

Said the editorial: "Just what business is it of ours . . . if young Americans leave home to escape the compulsion to fight in Vietnam?

"This is not a matter of taking one side or the other on the issue of Vietnam itself. What is at stake here is the right of political asylum—a right that we grant without hesitation to refugees from countries that we consider to be unfriendly, but a right equally valid for refugees from any country."

Washington's Warning

In Washington, Selective Service officials have warned in recent weeks that U.S. citizens who go to Canada to evade the draft will be prosecuted, and possibly drafted, when they return.

But Lieut. Gen. Lewis Hershey, U.S. draft director, told newsmen on a visit to Toronto last month that he is not worried about Canada's becoming a big haven for U.S. draft dodgers. Said General Hershey:

"I've got over 31 million men registered [for the draft] right now; I am not going to get excited about a few hundred. . . .

"If a boy violates our law, even by running to Canada, if he comes back to us and says, 'I'm ready to serve,' we would put him in the Army and not prosecute him."

CHRONOLOGY

January 10: The Georgia House of Representatives votes 184-12 to block state representative Julian Bond from serving his second term. Although the official charge is "disorderly conduct" (namely, Bond's opposition to the Vietnam War), racism also plays a role in the vote. Bond appeals the vote. In a unanimous ruling, the U.S. Supreme Court overturns the Georgia House's vote on the grounds that it violates Bond's First Amendment right to free speech.

January 17: A U.S. B-52 bomber collides with a fuel tanker while refueling over Palomares, Spain, destroying both planes and dropping four unarmed hydrogen bombs over the Spanish coastline. The bombs are recovered along with an estimated fourteen hundred tons of radiation-contaminated soil.

On the same day, folksingers Simon and Garfunkel release their album *Sounds of Silence.*

February 3: The Soviet unmanned probe *Luna 9* becomes the first spacecraft to land safely on the moon.

February 6–8: President Lyndon Johnson meets with incoming South Vietnamese premier Nguyen Cao Ky in Honolulu, Hawaii. The resulting Honolulu declaration expresses U.S. support for Ky's administration and a united effort to defeat the Vietcong and North Vietnamese invaders.

March 4: In an interview with the *London Evening Standard*, John Lennon remarks that the Beatles are "bigger than Jesus" in terms of popularity. The statement provokes outrage among American evangelicals, who organize massive boycotts and burn thousands of Beatles records in protest. Lennon later apologizes.

March 17: Union organizer Cesar Chavez leads a group of migrant farmworkers on a twenty-five-day march from Delano, California, to the steps of the state capitol in Sacramento in protest against unfair working conditions.

May 5: Steven B. Gray founds the Amateur Computer Society, the world's first organization of personal computer users.

May 29: Picketers opposed to the use of napalm, a chemical agent, in Vietnam begin protesting in front of the Dow Chemical Plant in Torrance, California, and its New York sales office. By the end of the year, fifty-five campus demonstrations and hundreds of smaller protests will be held in response to Dow's decision to continue manufacturing napalm for the government.

June 1–2: An estimated twenty-four hundred people attend a White House conference on civil rights.

June 2: The U.S. unmanned probe *Surveyor 1* becomes the second spacecraft to land safely on the moon.

June 2–9: At the 1966 Cold Spring Harbor Symposium, a group of biochemists led by future Nobel laureates Marshall Nirenberg and H. Gobind Khorana deliver a paper that cracks the "genetic code," revealing how information is stored in DNA.

June 5: James Meredith, the University of Mississippi's first African American student, begins a 220-mile "March Against Fear" from Memphis, Tennessee, to Jackson, Mississippi. He is shot en route and survives. Civil rights activists Martin Luther King Jr., Stokely Carmichael, and others resume the march in his place. After being arrested upon his arrival in Jackson, Carmichael coins the phrase "black power" in an angry speech condemning the Meredith shooting.

June 8: The National Football League (NFL) and the American Football League (AFL) announce plans for a merger, thereby creating the Super Bowl.

June 13: In *Miranda v. Arizona*, the U.S. Supreme Court rules that police officers must inform suspects of their rights before obtaining a binding confession.

July 1: France withdraws from the military structure of the North Atlantic Treaty Organization (NATO) to pursue its own nuclear weapons program.

July 4: President Lyndon Johnson signs the Freedom of Information Act into law, allowing private citizens and media outlets to obtain information on government activities.

July 13: Richard Speck murders eight Chicago nursing students.

August 1: Mentally ill ex-marine Charles Whitman shoots dozens of people from the balcony of the University of Texas's 307-foot Texas Tower; fourteen are killed.

August 3: Controversial stand-up comedian Lenny Bruce dies at age forty.

August 5: China's Communist Red Guard begins the Cultural Revolution, a violent ten-year effort to purge the nation's institutions of "imperialist" influences. An unknown number of Chinese citizens—at least several hundred thousand and possibly millions—will be killed.

August 10: The U.S. unmanned *Lunar Orbiter 1* searches the moon's surface for future landing sites.

August 29: The Beatles perform what would become their final live concert at Candlestick Park in San Francisco.

September 8: The first *Star Trek* episode airs on NBC.

September 12: The U.S. manned spacecraft *Gemini 11* practices space docking and takes photographs of Earth as a sphere.

October: Civil rights activists Huey P. Newton and Bobby Seale create the Black Panther Party.

October 6: California bans the hallucinogenic drug LSD.

October 24–25: President Lyndon Johnson meets with representatives from Australia, Korea, New Zealand, Philippines, South Vietnam, and Thailand in Manila, Philippines. The resulting Manila declaration of peace calls for peaceful resolution of the Vietnam War.

October 29: The National Organization for Women (NOW) is founded.

November 3: The Child Protection Act of 1966 bans M-80s, cherry bombs, and other particularly dangerous fireworks; limits the explosive power of other fireworks; and requires that all other flammable or combustible items be clearly labeled as such.

November 8: Ronald Reagan is elected governor of California.

December 16: The United Nations adopts the International Covenant on Civil and Political Rights and the International Covenant on Economic, Social, and Cultural Rights. Although the resolutions are not enforced, they affirm that citizens of all UN member states possess basic human rights that should be protected.

FOR FURTHER RESEARCH

Civil Rights

Stokely Carmichael and Charles V. Hamilton, *Black Power: The Politics of Liberation in America*. New York: Random House, 1967.

Richard W. Etulain, *César Chávez: A Brief Biography with Documents*. New York: Bedford/St. Martin's, 2002.

Susan Ferriss and Ricardo Sandoval, *The Fight in the Fields: Cesar Chavez and the Farmworkers Movement*. San Diego: Harvest Books, 1998.

Betty Friedan, *The Feminine Mystique*. New York: W.W. Norton, 2001.

——, *It Changed My Life: Writings on the Women's Movement*. New York: Random House, 1976.

Richard J. Jensen and John C. Hammerback, eds., *The Words of César Chávez*. College Station: Texas A&M University Press, 2002.

Charles Jones, *The Black Panther Party Reconsidered*. Baltimore, MD: Black Classic Press, 1998.

Jacques E. Levy, *Cesar Chavez: Autobiography of La Causa*. New York: W.W. Norton, 1975.

Peter Matthiessen, *Sal Si Puedes (Escape If You Can): Cesar Chavez and the New American Revolution*. Berkeley: University of California Press, 2000.

Huey P. Newton, *To Die for the People: The Writings of Huey P. Newton*. Ed. Toni Morrison. New York: Random House, 1995.

Ruth Rosen, *The World Split Open: How the Modern Women's Movement Changed America*. New York: Penguin, 2001.

Bobby Seale, *Seize the Time: The Story of the Black Panther Party and Huey P. Newton.* Baltimore, MD: Black Classic Press, 1997.

The Vietnam War

Michael S. Foley, *Confronting the War Machine: Draft Resistance During the Vietnam War.* Chapel Hill: University of North Carolina Press, 2003.

Sherry Gershon Gottlieb, ed., *Hell No, We Won't Go: Resisting the Draft During the Vietnam War.* New York: Viking, 1991.

John Hagan, *Northern Passage: American Vietnam War Resisters in Canada.* Cambridge, MA: Harvard University Press, 2001.

David Halberstam, *The Best and the Brightest.* New York: Ballantine, 1993.

George Herring, *America's Longest War: The United States and Vietnam 1950–1975.* Berkeley, CA: McGraw-Hill, 1995.

Neil Sheehan et al., eds., *The Pentagon Papers as Published by the* New York Times. New York: Quadrangle Books, 1971.

U.S. News & World Report, "Canada: Escape Hatch for U.S. Draft Dodgers," September 26, 1966.

Sports and Popular Culture

Jeff Miller, ed., *Going Long: The Wild Ten-Year Saga of the Renegade American Football League in the Words of Those Who Lived It.* Berkeley, CA: McGraw-Hill, 2003.

Leonard Nimoy, *I Am Not Spock.* Millbrae, CA: Celestial Arts, 1975.

Majel Barrett Roddenberry, "The Legacy of 'Star Trek,'" *Humanist*, July/August 1995.

William Shatner, *Star Trek Memories.* New York: HarperCollins, 1993.

Don Weiss, *The Making of the Super Bowl: The Inside Story of the World's Greatest Sporting Event.* Berkeley, CA: McGraw-Hill, 2002.

Stephen E. Whitfield and Gene Roddenberry, *The Making of Star Trek.* New York: Ballantine, 1968.

Crime, Justice, and Drugs

Liva Baker, *Miranda: Crime, Law, and Politics*. New York: Atheneum, 1983.

Dennis L. Breo and William J. Martin, *The Crime of the Century: Richard Speck and the Murder of Eight Nurses*. New York: Bantam, 1993.

Paula Chin et al., "An Unfathomable Evil," *People Weekly*, December 23, 1991.

Gary M. Lavergne, *A Sniper in the Tower: The Charles Whitman Murders*. Denton: University of North Texas Press, 1997.

Richard B. Leo and George C. Thomas III, eds., *The Miranda Debate: Law, Justice, and Policing*. Boston: Northeastern University Press, 1998.

David Nevin, "The Texas Sniper," *Life Magazine*, August 12, 1966.

Jay Stevens, *Storming Heaven: LSD and the American Dream*. New York: Grove Press, 1998.

Science and Technology

William E. Burrows, *This New Ocean: The Story of the First Space Age*. New York: Random House, 1999.

Paul Freiberger and Michael Swaine, *Fire in the Valley: The Making of the Personal Computer*. Berkeley, CA: McGraw-Hill, 1999.

Stephen B. Gray, "The Early Days of Personal Computers," *Creative Computing*, November 1984.

T.A. Heppenheimer, *Countdown: A History of Space Flight*. New York: John Wiley, 1999.

Sol Libes, "The First Ten Years of Amateur Computing," *Byte*, July 1978.

Homer E. Newell, "Surveyor: Candid Camera on the Moon," *National Geographic*, October 1966.

James Schefter, *The Race: The Complete True Story of How America Beat Russia to the Moon*. New York: Anchor, 2000.

Websites

A Huey P. Newton Story, www.pbs.org/hueypnewton. This exhaustive PBS companion site for the film *A Huey P. Newton Story* (2002), a drama-documentary directed by Spike Lee, features extensive information on the history of the Black Panther Party.

National Organization for Women, www.now.org. NOW is still a powerful force in American politics today, and its official website includes sections detailing its history and current activities.

United Farm Workers of America, www.ufw.org. The official website of the organization founded by Cesar Chavez features a detailed Chavez biography, a comprehensive history of the organization, and information on the upcoming Cesar E. Chavez Foundation website.

The Vietnam War Internet Project, www.vwip.org. Arguably the most comprehensive website of its kind, this massive directory features chronologies, articles, images, primary source documents, and other material pertaining to the Vietnam War.

INDEX